Long Time Coming!

**First Lesson Sermons For
Advent/Christmas/Epiphany**

Cycle A

Stephen M. Crotts

CSS Publishing Company, Inc., Lima, Ohio

LONG TIME COMING!

Copyright © 2001 by
CSS Publishing Company, Inc.
Lima, Ohio

Library of Congress Cataloging-in-Publication Data

Crotts, Stephen M.
    Long time coming! : first lesson sermons for Advent/Christmas/Epiphany, cycle A / Stephen M. Crotts.
        p. cm.
    ISBN 0-7880-1817-5 (alk. paper)
    1. Advent sermons. 2. Christmas sermons. 3. Epiphany season—Sermons. 4. Bible. O.T. Isaiah—Sermons. 5. Bible. O.T.—Sermons. 6. Sermons, American—21st century. I. Title.
BV4254.5 .C74 2001
252'.61—dc21   2001025078
                                                                                        CIP

For more information about CSS Publishing Company resources, visit our website at www.csspub.com.

ISBN 0-7880-1817-5   PRINTED IN U.S.A.

To the one person who
matters most in my life ...
Kathryn —
my wife of 28 years,
my friend,
my encourager,
my life-long love!

Table Of Contents

Foreword

It is not God's plan to take us by surprise ...

Throughout scripture there is the rolling thunder of Deity's voice: "I'm going to do it! Get ready! Pay close attention! Here comes what I promised!"

We call such predictions "prophecy," history written before it happens. And about nothing is God more prophetic, more predictive, than Jesus Christ.

"... a young woman shall conceive ..." (Isaiah 7:14).

"... his name shall be called Immanuel ..." (Isaiah 7:14).

"A bruised reed he will not break ..." (Isaiah 42:3).

Of all God's preachers, none was called more than Isaiah to herald the message of Christ's birth, life, and ministry. The Greeks prepared the language. Rome prepared the political peace, the roads. But it was Isaiah who stirred the hunger, the ancient longing for God's promised Messiah, the Divine intervention in human affairs.

And so it was to a very prepared stage in human history that Christ came.

This book, encompassing the church year, Cycle A, First Lessons for Advent, Christmas, and Epiphany, is an earnest attempt to proclaim by sermons something of the richness of Jesus' birth.

I humbly submit it to you that you may believe.

The Christmas Prophet

Isaiah. It's a strong name. A good Hebrew name. The "ah" sound evokes the sound of breath, of God's breath. The person who bore this label on his personhood would know Almighty God with face to face intimacy. Why, the name "Isaiah" literally means "God's salvation."

Theologians call Isaiah "The Christmas prophet." That's because of all the Old Testament prophets who foresaw the coming of the Messiah, Jesus, he, Isaiah, had the most to say about it all.

Isaiah was called to preach by the age of 25. The year was 765 B.C. In chapter six of his work he powerfully tells of his experience in the temple during which God seared his lips with a burning word. "Here am I! Send me!" Isaiah responded. And he went out to preach with fiery passion.

The office of a prophet in God's employ is a twofold labor. First, prophecy can mean to forth-tell God's Word to society. The most often repeated phrase in the Old Testament is "Thus saith the Lord."

Second, prophecy can mean to foretell the future. "It shall come to pass" is frequently on the lips of God's preachers.

After God ordained Isaiah a prophet, the Lord informed his man that his ministry would be largely fruitless. "Go, and say to his people: Hear and hear, but do not understand; see and see, but do not perceive.'" God was strengthening Isaiah's resolve to proclaim God's will to a truculent, stiff-necked people who were rushing headlong into ruin. Isaiah's job was simply to be able to say, "I told you so!"

Biblical history explains that Isaiah ministered for fifty years in southern Israel, in the region we call Judah and Jerusalem. Three kings reigned during his tenure as preacher: Jothan, Ahaz, and Hezekiah.

Reading the Christmas prophet is to discover a man who made his messages clear. He did it with memorable illustrations and remarkable poetic style.

Now, every life has a context. Just as Robert E. Lee generaled in the Civil War, so Isaiah's era, his time, is trenchant in understanding his message.

After kings David and Solomon, Israel as a nation was diminished in glory. There was disunity as the country split North and South. God began to be served half-heartedly. And corruption and injustice spread.

Not unlike our own nation today, Israel was a nation grown soft; material possessions were what mattered, and people became enthralled with self. God was small. The individual was large.

Suddenly, society was threatened by Assyria, a cruel, ruthless, marauding military power to the north. Utterly pagan, these warriors had humbled the Mideast from the Fertile Crescent to Egypt. They were known to slaughter their enemies with glee. Any prisoners of war were stripped bare, no matter if they were male or female.

Often the Assyrians put a fish hook in the cheeks of the prisoners of war. These hooks were then tied to a tether, and these human spoils of war were then jerked along in a procession of misery.

It was during the time of the Assyrian menace that Isaiah was ordained to speak with God to Israel. He became his nation's moral conscience, perhaps the greatest of all Israel's prophets.

How did Israel respond to Isaiah? Smug in their material wealth, secure in themselves, having reduced their relationship with God to a covenant of convenience, Israel turned a deaf ear to preaching and set to work trying to solve their problems without reference to God.

To fend off Assyria they formed military alliances with area kings. They hired mercenaries to bolster their army. They even provoked God's jealousy by resubmitting themselves to Egypt and the pharaoh, ignoring their national history and how God had brought them out years ago. It is a human tendency verified in the course of history. When we become our own moral standard, ultimately things go terribly wrong. But rather than repent and turn back to our creator God, we work harder, we throw money at our human woes, we seek a political solution.

Isaiah's job was to tell Israel, "If you lean on Egypt who once enslaved you, the same Egypt whose pharaoh God destroyed, from whom God brought you out in a mighty exodus never to return, if you lean on Egypt as a crutch, they will break like a stick and pierce you with a grievous wound!"

So it was Isaiah called God's people to repent of their waywardness, to return to God Almighty, to start living their creed once more.

Israel refused.

What Isaiah did next is amazing. He married and fathered two sons. The names he gave his boys were prophetic. It goes to show the lengths some preachers will go to be heard, to get their point across! Son number one was called Shear-Jashub which translated, "The remnant will return." The second was called Maher-Shalal-Hash-Baz, "The shame is imminent."

More of Isaiah's life is recorded in the second book of Kings.

Outlining Isaiah's preaching is easy, for he was a clear, organized author who wrote things down. His outline is as follows:

1. The covenanting Holy God of Israel is!
2. We are his people, and we've grown slack in keeping his covenant.
3. God is judging us with Assyria.
4. We cannot fix things up ourselves. Alliance, money, human endeavor are false hopes.
5. Return to the covenant now in repentance and obedience.
6. Since you won't repent, my two sons' names say it all: "The shame is imminent" — war, conquest, nudity, fish hooks in your jaws. And "The remnant will return" after a punishing exile.

7. Now Isaiah (some say it was his assistant) turns from scalding prophetic doom words to tender-hearted pastoral eloquence. Isaiah 40:1: "Comfort, comfort my people ... speak tenderly ... cry to her ... her warfare is ended."
8. The final portion of Isaiah's message is not forth-telling, but foretelling. He speaks and writes of the coming one, the Messiah, the Savior Jesus:

"A young woman shall conceive" (Isaiah 7:14).

"The people who walked in darkness have seen a great light" (Isaiah 9:2).

"For to us a child is born, to us a son is given; and the government will be upon his shoulder, and his name shall be called Wonderful Counselor, Mighty God, Everlasting Father, Prince of Peace" (Isaiah 4:6).

Years later, in the mid-1700s, a German-born composer living in Great Britain, a man known as George Friedrich Handel, a Christian, used the prophet Isaiah's words as the foundation for his now famous Christmas oratorio, *Messiah*. It is performed in every major city almost worldwide each December. So Isaiah's message still speaks. He calls us to the Christ — once a Baby — now a Savior — soon a Judge!

Still Small Voice

Ask any child at Christmas!

There are three ways to look at a Christmas package. The first is to look forward to it. This is best accomplished by squeezing it, shaking it, and guessing its contents by its weight. The second is to open it. Here, anticipation turns to knowledge as layers of wrapping paper, tape, and tissue are torn away and the contents laid bare. And finally there is the memory stage. This happens when you take the gift out of the box and put it on or put it to use over the years of your life and experience just what it can do.

In the Bible we have these same three perspectives of Christ's birth. There were those who looked forward to his coming. They were the prophets — Isaiah, Hosea, Micah, Balaam, and the like. Seeing Christmas from afar, they predicted his virgin birth, his nativity at Bethlehem, and even his death on the cross.

Then there were those who looked on Christmas. The events of the nativity were literally unwrapped right before their eyes. Such was the experience of Mary and Joseph, Herod, shepherds, wise men, Anna, and Simeon.

And finally, there were those who looked back on Christmas. Men like Paul wrote of the meaning of Christ's birth with an understanding born of years of experience.

Our text today comes from the first perspective, the prophetic. It is an oracle of the prophet Isaiah in which an ideal king is anticipated. And in it the seer beholds Christ from afar. There is a dim outline of salvation; none of the details are filled in, but, nonetheless, Christ is foreseen.

When Isaiah wrote this text, Israel was experiencing a gloomy political existence. From the unity and military prowess of King David's era, the Jews had fallen. Corruption, injustice, and disobedience had toppled the nation. Now Israel was being constantly invaded, conquered, and downtrodden by foreigners. In chapter 10 Isaiah symbolizes Israel as a once proud forest cut down to stumps by the wrath of God.

And now in chapter 2 he turns from judgment to hope, from punishment to deliverance. And this is what he says, "There shall come forth a shoot from the stump of Jesse, and a branch shall grow out of his roots." Let's get into this prophecy and see what it has for us this Christmas.

Hurt

First of all, the prophecy of Isaiah tells us that there is hurt in Christmas. It gives us the symbol of a stump. Once mighty Israel is now cut down and carried away. Only the stump remains.

You'll have to agree that a stump is one of the most hopeless-looking things in all the world. It is quite a come-down from the heights of a mature tree. Where once a tall whispering giant stood providing shade and fruit, now there is only a stump, ugly and dead-looking.

In the Old Testament, when a nation invaded and conquered Israel, quite often they would capture the king and his sons alive. The sons would then be slain in front of the king and then the king himself would be tortured by having his eyes gouged out. The last thing he would ever see then would be his boys' deaths. Next the king's hands would be cut off or his tongue cut out or even his feet crippled. And this poor stump of a man would then be deported and forced to live among his conquerors as a symbol of their international dominance, a living reminder of his failure and their success, a trophy of despair.

It's that type of world, isn't it? There are those in our day who have been cut down in divorce. Their spouse, the courts, have lopped off income, home, children, furniture, friends, and even hope. Where once Christmas meant marriage, children, a fire in the hearth, laughter and feasting and exchanging gifts, now there is only a stump — a cold half-furnished apartment with a telephone that never rings.

A businessman in the city told me he once had a car dealership with 300 cars to choose from, 27 full-time employees, and customers who'd been loyal to his trust for 25 years! But as he drove along on his way to his new job as an assistant manager in an outlet, he pointed to a vacant lot, windswept and fallen into disrepair. "It was all swept away in the recession, all swept into bankruptcy," he explained. Again, a stump. A living reminder of what once was and what now isn't.

From divorce courts to bankruptcy, Isaiah's vision of an entire nation that has been leveled like a clear-cut forest does not miss our own nation very far. The quality of education in our public schools continues to slump. Then there are the stumps of Vietnam and Watergate, and of course, the stump of good service. Remember how at the gas station they not only used to pump your gas but also wipe your windows and check the oil and tire pressure, too? But that's all gone now. And so many of our once productive factory towns now rust in idleness. Our prisons run full. Our churches are half full. And whole segments of the inner city are kept alive by the hope of another heroin fix or six-pack.

Is there a stump in your life? Some broken friendship? A once vibrant health now cut down? A dream now broken? So it was. So it was in Isaiah's day. And so it now is. But don't miss this!

Happiness

Not only does Isaiah's Christmas vision contain a symbol of despair, the stump, but also it has in it a symbol of joy and that symbol is the "root."

The text says, "There shall come forth a shoot from the stump of Jesse, and a branch shall grow out of his roots."

Some quick explaining here: King David's father was Jesse. And God promised someone from Jesse's and David's lineage would always rule Israel. The people clung to this promise even when all Israel was overrun and ruined by Assyria, Babylon, and others. "God has promised. He will keep His word. He will give us

15

a new David! Where is Jesse's next son, our new king and deliverer, who will build Israel back?"

The text here is also playing on our knowledge of a phenomena that might not be all that familiar to us today. Have you ever noticed how a tree that is chopped down will often sprout again from its stump and grow a new tree? As long as there is life in the roots there is hope for a new beginning. Just add moisture, sunlight, and time and a new tree will grow every bit as grand as the first. This is the symbol of happiness Isaiah shares with a fallen nation. "From the roots of the stump a shoot has burst forth!"

It also helps to see that in scripture a root is a symbol of many positive things. The word "root" can mean "stability" (Colossians 2:7), "strength" (Isaiah 14:30), "the cause of something" (1 Timothy 6:10), "a foundation" (Job 28:9), "parents" (Daniel 11:7), and even "Jesus Christ" (Isaiah 11:10, Revelation 5:5).

So, Isaiah looks at the stump of his nation, the stumps of the lives of the people around him, and from his lips comes a word of happiness. "I see a root," he cries. "I can see new growth! There is life yet!"

There are still people of vision like that among us today, are there not? People who can see in old junk a priceless antique. People who can see in a rusty old car a restorable collector's item. And from ruin they can bring new life.

One such man of our time was George Marshall. After World War II Europe lay in ruins, its youth slain in combat, its economy shattered, its cities smoking rubble. General George Marshall decided it was time to spend as much time and energy and money making peace in Europe as had been done making war. His plan to rebuild Europe became known as the Marshall Plan. And during the decade of its implementation Europe grew from a stump to a tall tree. And this is what Isaiah says God is doing in the world during Israel's day, during Christ's day, during our day every day.

No matter how cut-down we are, no matter our sin, God is here and on his mind is a plan to spend more effort bringing redemption and new life than Satan and man have in bringing sin and death. And God, the Bible says, has more life than we have death. He has more forgiveness than we have sin.

The Good News is that in the stump of man's existence there is a root, always the root! There is in us a stability, a strength, a foundation, a hidden cause, a divine Father, a Christ — and from this root shall come a shoot, and from that shoot a sapling, and from that a tree!

Now, granted, a root would seem to be small cause for joy. But look at it this way: If you had a favorite houseplant that got knocked to the floor and broken off at the stump you would mourn. But when you saw new life coming from the stump weeks later, you'd take joy knowing that one day your plant would be restored to you.

In a way Jesus, as a direct descendant of David and Jesse, was not much to look at, a small occasion for joy. Isaiah said of him in 53:2: "He grew up before him like a young plant, and like a root out of dry ground; he had no form or comeliness that we should look at him, and no beauty that we should desire him." Jesus' birth for most people went entirely unnoticed. He was just one more peasant child born, another mouth to feed, another baby destined to grow into an adult, do his allotted tasks, die, and find his place in obscurity.

Yet, my, my! Look at how his root has grown! It is a fact of history that fewer than one out of a million people is famous. And most people who are famous achieve their fame during their lifetime. Then, after their death, their fame begins to fade as history writes their worth in fewer and fewer paragraphs.

Yet with Jesus Christ we have one of the true ironies of history, for with him the exact opposite is true! Christ, you see, was born in poverty, reared in obscurity, ministered during a brief three years to at most 500 ardent followers, and was literally crossed out by the powers that be, dying the death of a convicted felon. Yet, instead of quickly fading into obscurity like others, his name has brightened and gathered momentum and risen to the point where no other name among men is given more space in the encyclopedia of history.

Hope

So, Christmas is part hurt, for there is a stump; indeed, there are stumps in our lives. And Christmas is part happiness, because there is a root, a new beginning, a coming king, a restoration begun. And this leads us to the latter part of the text which points us to the future. Isaiah predicts, "There shall come forth a shoot from the stump of Jesse, and a branch shall grow out of his roots. And the Spirit of the Lord shall ..." That's future tense, isn't it? Isaiah is saying, "It might look like a stump to you right now, but look ahead! God is at work. Life is here."

When some things are cut off they don't grow back — arms, legs, fingers. But tree limbs grow back, vines and blossoms, too. And Isaiah is saying that in the Spirit of God, in Jesus Christ, there is no hurt God will not heal, no loss God will not restore.

Take the root of Jesus Christ himself. From the stump of Israel came a new shoot. It grew into a tree. And man chopped it down, fashioned it into a cruel cross, and nailed Jesus there to die. But God made that cross the root of our salvation and raised Jesus from the dead in triumph!

And this same God who did all that for Jesus is still at work doing the same for the widow, the prisoner, the orphan, the sick and suffering, the bankrupt, the divorced, and the failed. You've but to reach out to him by faith and he is there!

And what's more, the text says this new life is not just growing up among us to inspire. It is growing up to rule. Isaiah 11:1-10 says the spirit will be upon Christ — wisdom, might, fair judgment, the ability to rule. In him, the earth will become a new garden of Eden where roots flourish, where harm ceases, and harmony prevails. The nations of the world will come to stare in amazement at what has grown out of Jesse's stump!

The only suicide note I've ever seen said this: "My family is gone. My business is wrecked. My feelings are numb. I can't see the future. There is within me no tiny reason for hope. Good-bye." Yet to this man and to you and to me Isaiah points to a tiny root. And never underestimate the power of a tiny hope!

Note, if you will, the emphasis in the text on the little things. Small stumps. Little roots. Tiny shoots. This is an emphasis carried throughout the entire Christmas theme. And it is true to the nature of God who speaks in a "still small voice." There is but a single small star, no banner headline, to guide the wise men to

Bethlehem, itself a small town. Mary and Joseph are but wee peasant people in the eyes of the world, hailing themselves from the tiny town of Nazareth. The innkeeper's hotel is so small it cannot accommodate another threesome. Christ was born a tiny baby in a tiny town within a tiny nation. Of Jesus, John the Baptizer would say, "He must increase, but I must decrease." And that is exactly what has been happening in the scheme of things!

Remember the first Saul of the Bible? His Hebrew name means, "One who is big in his own sight." And wasn't King Saul tall and handsome, big in the flesh, yet short in the spirit in obedience? Such is man. But then Christ was born. The root of Jesse began to grow. And the New Testament tells of another Saul born and converted to Christ and nicknamed "Paul," which is Latin for "shorty." But this Saul, though short in stature, was to loom large spiritually by evangelizing Europe and Asia Minor and writing much of the New Testament. Such is the role of Christ! And such is our hope.

Conclusion

Has there been sin in your life? Has the year brought pain and struggle and left you with but a stump? Isaiah looked into all of this and called a stump a stump. But he anticipated what God would do as well. Stirred by the Holy Spirit he set the theme of Christmas that would inspire joy and hope for all time. For in Christ, from tragedy, from the ugly, the unnoticed, the unwanted and forgotten, comes new life, opportunity, a fresh start.

Many years ago I was given an odd gift. It came from a college friend and I thought at first that it was a practical joke. You see, when I opened the package I found nothing but a dried-up plant. Included was a small card that simply said, "Please don't throw me away. I really am a beautiful 'Star of Bethlehem' plant. Just place me in a dark place, water me, and wait." So I did. And in two weeks the plant began to come alive. When I placed it in my window, blossoms of yellow and white, and touches of blue burst forth. There all the time in that dead-looking plant a beauty was stirring, a root of life just waiting to spring forth! And it is just the same with us and God. For within each of us in Christ there is a root stimulated by faith, nourished by worship, watered by obedience, inspired by the Holy Spirit. And it will grow if we but allow it. This is the gift of God! A gift that might seem at first to be a joke. But, nonetheless, a gift with life in it.

To be sure, Christmas is part hurt: "the stump." It is also part happiness: "the root." But it is all hope! "He shall ..." For God only knows what your root in Christ can grow into.

Why not water the spirit of Christmas in your life and wait?

What Good Music
Can Do For You

It is a scientific fact that when the music of Mozart is played in a henhouse, chickens lay more eggs. This particular sermon was written to the tune of Mozart's piano concertos, so if it seems to have a lot of "strut" and "cluck," you'll know why! Seriously, if music can do that for hens, what can good music do for you?

Isaiah predicted that when God redeems a people they become singers! Music begins to flow from their lips! "And the ransomed of the Lord shall return, and come to Zion with singing" (35:10). And certainly the Christmas season of the year proves this to be true!

Judaism and Christianity are two of the only major world religions that have a hymnal. That's because in Christ we have something to sing about!

In Acts 16:25 there is an entertaining tale about music. "... but about midnight Paul and Silas were praying and singing hymns to God, and the prisoners were listening," offers a clue as to the role music played in the lives of the early Christians. And you can be sure music today offers the same ministries to you.

Composure, Comfort

One of the first roles music played in Paul's life was to give composure, relaxation, and a sense of serenity. Paul, the gallant spiritual warrior, and Silas, his traveling companion, had become embroiled in conflict. They had been publically stripped and beaten and thrown into the stockade. Life had crashed in upon them. The future was clouded with despair. So Paul and Silas began to sing. From deep within their soul a melody surfaced and found its voice in a hymn. Note carefully what is going on here! Two men in a disharmonious world are with their voices imposing a bit of harmony on their situation.

A clue to the nature and importance of music is found in the fact that music is first mentioned in Genesis, chapter four, of the Bible. In Genesis, chapter two, we are told of the harmony in the Eden paradise. In chapter three that harmony is destroyed by sin and judgment. And then music appears! Genesis 4:21 introduces Jubal, the father of all those who make music. It is as if God is giving the human race a balm for this cacophonous world we must live in. It's as if he knew we'd be homesick for Eden's orderliness, so God gave us music, a human habit of imposing order and harmony on the noisy world. And the result of making music is to gain a deeper sense of peace, a deeper sense of what the world was in Eden and shall be in the kingdom when it comes. And it is to be comforted.

This is what Paul and Silas were reaching for when they were imprisoned. And this is what they found in music.

It is said that Martin Luther, the church reformer of the 1500s, used to get terribly spent and depressed with his efforts. And it was at such times that he would say to those around him, "Let's go sing Psalm 96!" And the sounds of "A Mighty Fortress Is Our God" would fill the room. In my own life I know of the value such good music can play. I constantly see the disharmony of broken marriages, the clash of different theologies and tastes and races, the pain of grief. And many a day I come home weary with it all. That's when I turn on the music of Vivaldi. And after letting his music sweep over my soul in wave after wave of splendid harmony, I feel like there is hope and meaning in life once again. He reaches inside me and puts everything back in its place. And I am comforted. That's what good music can do for you!

Worship

The second gift of music is worship. Music can help you worship God.

Paul and Silas began to pray and sing a hymn about midnight. They were worshiping Christ and using a hymn to do it.

A clear principle of scripture is that God acts and the people flee the realm of prose to music in order to respond. When Moses crossed the Red Sea and the pursuing Egyptians were destroyed, Moses broke into song, "I will sing unto the Lord for he has triumphed gloriously, the horse and rider he has thrown into the sea" (Exodus 15:11). When Mary was told she would mother the Christ child she broke into a hymn, "My soul doth magnify the Lord ..." (Luke 1:46). The phenomena is there throughout the Bible — God acts and his people sing it!

Christianity is one of the only major religions in the world that has a hymn book. The simple fact of the matter is we've got something to sing about! God has acted! In Jesus Christ's life, death, and resurrection God has acted! And our response down through the ages has been the music of psalms, doxologies, Gregorian chants, hymns, requiems, and cantatas.

Karl Barth put it so well when he said, "Words are hostile to the genuine miracle of Christmas: detrimental, always powerless to justify it. How fortunate that when we are disturbed and oppressed by the problem of words we can flee to the realm of music ... music is the true and legitimate bearer of the message of Christmas." And so it is!

But did you know that humans are not the only part of creation to make music? The Bible tells us that the birds and trees and winds and brooks all sing the praises of God (Isaiah 55:12). The book of Revelation tells us that the angels in heaven sing to God (Revelation 4:10-11). When Jesus entered Jerusalem triumphantly, the people met him with hosanna songs of joy! And the pharisees said, "Master, rebuke your followers for such praises!" But Jesus answered, "I tell you, if these were silent the very stones would cry out!" Nature sings! Angels sing! And when we sing, we join in a great cosmic choir that has praised God endlessly from all creation! (This would make an interesting discussion the next time someone asks how big a choir you sing in!)

In western Virginia there is a church building right next to a prison. And on Sunday morning people in both places worship God. The singing in the church is dull and half-hearted. But the singing in the prison fellowship is loud and joyful. "Preacher," the man is often asked, "how do you explain the difference?" And the truth is that God has acted in Christ for those prisoners. And they are responding with musical joy. But for the church members? Well, perhaps they've been too busy, too self-contented, to feel any need for God. Whatever, I tell you, there is something very wrong with a person who does not sing. Why, if you don't have to praise God, you haven't met him yet! That's what good music will do to you!

Inspiration

A third role music can play in our lives is inspiration. Paul and Silas were in a low spot in their lives. They were helpless, hurting, and in prison. And it is a natural human tendency to allow the environment to dictate our mood. Why, one in Paul's predicament could easily be expected to get depressed. And so it was that Paul fled to the realm of music to bolster both his and Silas' morale.

Have you ever noticed how the military uses band music to give morale to its troops? The rousing music of John Philip Sousa is worth an entire battalion when it comes to its effect on the men.

Franz Joseph Haydn in a letter to a friend said that when he wrote music, the voice of God within him whispered, "There are but few contented and happy people here below. Everywhere grief and care prevail. Perhaps your labor may one day be the source from which the weary and worn, or the person burdened with affairs, may derive a few moments of rest and refreshment." And he has left us symphonies, any one of which can do much to inspire you, lift your morale, and give you courage to conquer!

Notice with me in 1 Samuel 16:14-26 how young David used the music of stringed instruments to soothe a very troubled King Saul.

Notice in Matthew 26:30 how Christ sang a hymn with his disciples just after the Last Supper. Was it partly to lift his morale on the way to the garden and the trial and the cross?

I tell you, these principles of music are as ancient as the Old Testament. And the world is onto them! Hitler used Sousa marches in World War II. Notice how they play inspiring music in a dental office, a shopping mall, and even in an office! And it's high time we Christians realize what good music can do, as well!

Witness

So, what can good music do for you? It can comfort you, help you worship, and inspire you. And now a final principle. Music can help you witness.

Paul and Silas were in jail, and they were not alone. The jailer was nearby. Other inmates were about. And when Paul and Silas began to vocalize their faith with music, the others listened and questioned in their hearts, "Why are they singing? What does this mean? Who is this Christ? How can they have joy in this lousy jail?"

How often we are tongue-tied when it comes to expressing our deepest convictions. But when words fail, music can speak!

In Mexico a bashful lover can hire a small band with singers to serenade his true love. A popular American love song a few years back said "Every time I try to say I love you the words just come out wrong, so I have to say I love you in a song."

Yes, music can witness to our deepest convictions.

A few years ago I had a particularly hard day. I was suffering with a chronic backache. Several severe disappointments had come my way in people. My wife had wrecked the car. A thief had stolen my lawn mower and bicycles. There was a mountain of laundry waiting at the newly repaired washing machine. And three pre-school children seemed to have more energy than they deserved. And, oh boy! Was I ever grouchy! I sulked. I fussed. I slammed doors. I stomped around the house barking orders. Wow! I was breaking every single rule I ever wrote or preached about! (Feel better now?) Well, I finally ended up glowering on the back porch steps while my wife kept a safe distance in the kitchen where she was washing dishes. And do you know what she was doing? She was singing! "Fairest Lord Jesus," "Victory In Jesus," "This is My Father's World," and "Glorious Things Of Thee Are Spoken" all came floating out the window to me. And as the music washed over me I began to soften, to relax, and to become more receptive to the Lord's work within my life. Again, the value of good music proved its ability to witness, to penetrate despair with the good news that Jesus is the Christ.

And isn't that what happened as Paul and Silas sang of Jesus? The jailer heard and began to consider God.

Note, too, that the Bible says, "Make a joyful noise unto the Lord" (Psalm 100). It doesn't tell us we have to sing well. It just says be noisy and joyful! And that's how Paul and Silas must have sounded, because there was an earthquake at the sound of their music. And, well, one thing led to another and the jailer and his household became Christians.

That's what good music can do for you!

Are You Deaf?

Did you hear about the university professor of music who retired and went to Africa to prove his theory that music soothes the savage beast? He set up his cello in a clearing and began to make music. Soon a zebra and a gorilla stood watching. Next came the antelope, a lion, several tigers, and a monkey. They all stood listening, fascinated. But suddenly a panther came bounding out of the jungle, leaped upon the man, and ate him. Angrily the lion demanded, "What did you do that for?" To which the panther turned his deaf ear and said, "How's that again?"

Too many of us Christians have been deaf when it comes to good music. Oh, we listen to bad music or only country music, or no music at all. And we miss out on the fact that what music did for Paul and Silas it can still do for us today, if we but open up to it.

Paul had no stereo. He had no portable radio, no cassette tape player in his car. He did not have the advantages we do of Isaac Watts or Johann Sebastian Bach, or of the piano, the French horn, or the violin, or of contemporary Christian music. And still music ministered powerfully in his life comforting, aiding in worship, inspiring, and witnessing. And how much more can it accomplish in us today?

We have it on the good authority of Dorothy Parker that life is a banquet, and yet some of us poor suckers are starving to death! Well, no more! In Jesus Christ we have something to sing about! And I challenge you from God's Word today to let music work its ministry in your life! Then shall the prophecy of Isaiah 35:10 be further fulfilled: "And the ransomed of the Lord shall return, and come to Zion with singing."

Now Playing:
God, Live And In Person!

Some years ago I was in a London theater watching a Harold Pinter play. The drama was not very good really. I was getting bored. Then right in the middle of the play the theater manager walked on stage, excused himself, and made an announcement. The actors stared. The audience looked shocked. Me? I thought it was all part of the play. Such interruptions are rare in a theater. But nonetheless, the stage manager felt that it was necessary this time. His announcement was nothing trivial like, "Some owner has left his car lights on." Nor was it a terrifying message like, "Fire! Fire! Clear the house!" Instead he quietly asked, "Is there a doctor in the house?" One of the stage hands had had a heart attack and needed medical attention.

Christmas is like this episode because this is the time when God gets into the drama of history. This play, this earthly drama, I might add, is not a very good act either. It's too bloody, too boring; it lacks character. And right in the middle of things the divine producer, the director of the universe, God Almighty Himself, steps onto the stage to make an announcement. His statement is neither trivial nor terrifying. It's good news. "For to you is born this day in the city of David a Savior, who is Christ the Lord" (Luke 2:11).

Matthew 1:23 tells us something about the God who interrupts. We are told something about the Lord who enters the picture at Christmas. The verse says, " 'His name shall be called Emmanuel,' (which means, God with us)." This is at least part of the overall statement that God interrupts history to make each

Christmas. He is saying, "You are not alone now. I am with you. Emmanuel."

In the popular cultic religion of transcendental meditation, each person is given a mantra. The mantra is a secret word that is usually meaningless. The individual meditates by focusing all his attention on this secret word. If it all seems like a waste of time, that's because it usually is. Christianity also offers meditation, but our mantra is no secret, and it certainly is not meaningless. Our "mantra" is Emmanuel. He is our object of mental focus. As Isaiah the Prophet said, "Thou dost keep him in perfect peace, whose mind is stayed on thee, because he trusts in thee" (Isaiah 26:3).

As one meditates, "stays one's mind," on the fact of Christmas, Emmanuel, it becomes obvious that "God with us" holds great significance for all of life. In fact, one way of looking at the entire New Testament is to see it as a long meditation on the Lord's being with us in the world.

God With Us To Teach
Truly God is with us in many ways. But one of the important ways that he is with us is in teaching. Jesus Christ came to teach us. God promised, "I will instruct you and teach you the way you should go" (Psalm 32:8). At Christmas Jesus came to fulfill that pledge.

Most of you know how large many of our colleges and universities are getting. Some classes may have several hundred students. The professor often never even comes to class. His lectures are beamed in over closed circuit television. He has no personal contact with his students. It is all but impossible to get an appointment with him. And when you get your grade it is not hand-lettered but computer punched. Many people feel God is like that professor. He is aloof. He's some sort of cold and calculating celestial computer that grades humankind. Thank God that Christmas disproves this theory. God is not distant. He is available! Emmanuel, God is with us! This is the message of Christmas. The Lord did not teach us by giving us a lecture or a song or a book or a tape recording. He came himself. "The Word became flesh and dwelt among us" (John 1:14).

In 1928 a young mechanic was working on his A-Model Ford car. He couldn't get it to run. He had checked the battery, cleaned the engine, and tightened the starter. Nonetheless, his car would not run. Disgusted, the would-be mechanic threw down his wrench and sat on the running board. About then a nice new shiny Ford pulled up. Out stepped a well-dressed man who looked into the motor and said, "I see you're having a little difficulty with your car. If you'll adjust the carburetor this way your car will run." The carburetor was adjusted, the car cranked, and, lo and behold, it sprang to life! The mechanic was amazed! He turned to the stranger and said, "Just who are you anyway, mister?" The man said, "The name's Ford, my boy — Henry Ford. I made that car. I ought to know what makes it run!" Now the gospel story is that the very God of all creation, the God who made you, put in all the plumbing and the wiring, came down to this earth on Christmas day to tap you on the shoulder and say, "If it's not working, listen to me! I put you together. I can make you work abundantly!"

Emmanuel — God with us to teach. Do you want to learn? Are you teachable? When the pupil is willing, the teacher comes! Do you want to learn how to live? Jesus said, "I have come that you might have life and have it more abundantly!" Do you want to learn how to pray? Jesus taught us the Lord's Prayer. Do you want to know what God is like? Jesus said, "He who has seen me has seen the Father." Do you want to learn how to suffer? Look at Jesus' lifestyle. He knew rejection, criticism, and crucifixion. Would you like to learn how to witness? See how Jesus shared with the woman at the well. And yes, if you want to learn how to die, study the Lord's death on the cross.

With Us To Suffer

Emmanuel, God with us to teach. "I will instruct you and teach you," God promised. And Emmanuel fulfilled it. But the significance of Emmanuel doesn't end with teaching. The Lord is also with us to suffer.

Remember the nursery rhyme, "Solomon Grundy"? "Solomon Grundy, born on Monday, christened on Tuesday, married on

Wednesday, took ill on Thursday, worse on Friday, died on Saturday, buried on Sunday. This is the end of Solomon Grundy." Mr. Grundy's story is every man's story. We all hurt. We are all bruised by rejection, loneliness, and alienation. We all get sick, suffer, and die. But as the creed says, "Jesus Christ was born of the virgin Mary, suffered under Pontius Pilate, was crucified, dead, and buried." He suffers what we suffer. Job, amidst his agony, asked a question of God that we all well might ask. "Hast thou eyes of flesh? Dost thou see as man sees?" (Job 10:4). We have our answer in Emmanuel. God is with us in suffering.

Growing up, I worked in my father's furniture store. One of the things I remember most about my dad was that he never asked me to do anything that he wouldn't do himself. When we were unloading a truck, he was right there. When we were pulling inventory from a hot, dusty warehouse, he was shoulder to shoulder with us. He put in the same hours and pulled the same load we did. Christmas is a reminder that God is with us like this, too. He has not asked us to do or endure anything that he hasn't lived through himself.

A black man died and went to heaven. He got with several of his race and they started comparing life histories. Finally, they approached God and their spokesman said, "You just don't realize how tough it was down there! I was born black. I was of a despised race!" And God said, "I was once a Jew." The man went on, "Yea, but I was persecuted. My daddy was innocent, but still the KKK hanged him." And Jesus showed him his nail-scarred hands. "You don't understand, Lord!" the black man went on. "I never had a cent, no education, no home. People laughed and scoffed at me. Why, when I was a baby, we had to flee our home and move to another city for the safety of our lives." And God smiled tenderly. He placed his big arm around the black man's shoulder and he said, "I know how it is, my son. I have been there myself."

With Us To Save!

Emmanuel — God with us. He is with us to teach. He is with us to suffer. What we feel, he has felt as well. But the meditation doesn't end here. He is with us for more. He is here to save. Jesus said, "The Son of Man came to save the lost" (Matthew 18:11).

A cartoon in a popular magazine showed a shepherd looking at Mary and Joseph and their baby and saying, "Poor kid. What a terrible time to be born." Things haven't changed that much either. It's still a tough world to be born into. There is crime, divorce, inflation, the threat of war, injustice, alcoholism, cancer, pollution — what a terrible time for a child to be born! But my, my! What a perfect time for Christ to be born. He is with us to save us. And do we ever need salvation!

Each Christmas we are accustomed to chopping down a live tree, dragging it into our homes, and decorating it. The tree looks all so festive. People marvel at it. "Beautiful," they say. But examine it more closely. It is already starting to dry out and turn brown. It is shedding its needles. It's really dead. People are like Christmas trees, too. They are actually dead. They are cut off from God, their sap and roots. They are slowly drying up. But rather than admit it, everyone tries to fake it by hanging colorful ornaments all over themselves — country club, diplomas, fine clothes, big automobiles. Inside they are dead and hurting, but on the outside they are putting on a good show. Yet it's all to no avail. There comes a time when the tree is stripped of all its lights and ornamentation and it is carried outside and thrown away.

But Jesus Christ came to change all that! He came to get you connected back up to your roots in God. He came to give you new sap and green. If you listen to him and follow his plan you won't have to fake it. You will really be alive. You will really feel alive. You won't be growing stale and brown, but green and fresh! What is your decision concerning a savior this Christmas? Do you want to fake life or have the fact of life?

God Is With Us! Are You With God?

Yes, Jesus Christ is our Emmanuel. God is now with us. He has broken into the drama of Christmas to teach us, to suffer with us, and to save us. But the meditation doesn't stop here. Christmas is not the end. It is only the beginning. In the year ahead we will see how God is with us in every part of our lives. He is with us in

31

our marriages and in our money. He is with us in the rearing of our children and our children's children. He is with us when we study and cry and work and play. Emmanuel is his name. It means God with us.

Touring around Virginia you will notice many historical markers that inform you of some great man's or woman's past activity in the area. "George Washington slept here." "Patrick Henry lived here." "Woodrow Wilson was born here." "The Civil War ended here." Today we have something of the same. Only we do not have a marker pointing out some past historical event. It is rather a statement of current events. "Emmanuel," we are told. "God is with us." Not, "God slept here," or "God was here but he didn't like it and he left," but, "God is with us."

Now do you see why the title of this sermon reads, "Now Playing: God, Live And In Person"? The Lord God, the Creator, the Almighty Judge, the Sustainer and Savior of the world, is right here in our midst. He has broken into history. He has joined the drama. He's on stage live and in person.

The fact is — God is with us. The question is — How do we respond?

The Taste Of Joy!

When traveling to Israel, Jerusalem is the place! But if you arrive on the weekend, it might not seem so. You see, Friday is the Muslim holy day and everything Arab is closed. Saturday is the Jewish holy day. So everything Jewish is shut tight. Then Sunday is the Christian day of rest and things Christian are closed. So, if you arrive in Jerusalem on a weekend, you'll find it a very quiet place for three days.

There are those who love it, though — the men on the tour — for Jerusalem on the weekend means three entire days without shopping. But things can get boring if one finds history, architecture, geography, and long walks dull. After all, it is the people who make Israel exciting — crowded streets, a babble of languages, music and laughter, milling crowds in the marketplace, and the smell of exotic foods cooking in the numerous roadside stands.

The first few times I went to Israel I ended up in Jerusalem on weekends. And I came to view people there as taking their religion far too seriously. Black robes. Somber faces. Fasting. The Wailing Wall. Music in a minor key. Closed doors. Yet I've been to Israel enough times now to know where to go to find the fun on weekends. Saturday night after sunset the Sabbath ends. And if you look, you can find a wedding somewhere with its accompanying feast and dancing in the streets. Or Saturday morning at the Wailing Wall there is joy afoot as Jewish boys, twelve year olds, become sons of the Covenant at their bar mitzvahs. And if that's not enough for you, at the YMCA on the weekends there is the "Sobra," a festival of Jewish folk dancing and costumes.

The first time I discovered such dancing, feasting, singing, and joy, I must admit, I was caught completely off guard. For I had not realized Jews were such a joyous people.

Voltaire wrote, "God is like a comedian playing to a crowd that is afraid to laugh." Ten years ago my approach to the Old Testament was like that. It was such a forbidding book of prophetic doom, death, and justice all under the watchful eye of a stern, holy God. People were afraid to laugh.

And the New Testament wasn't all that different. Christians were such a serious, gloomy, dull people talking all the time about sin, coming judgment, the cross, and repentance. They spoke of a God with a frowning countenance, a great tribulation and beasts, anti-Christs, and Armageddons. And when one goes into today's church one finds more of the same, Christians desperately concerned about famine somewhere, injustice, nuclear war, ecology, abortion, and pornography.

But suddenly, in Jerusalem, I discovered Christians and Jews dancing in the streets, feasting, and making merry with all their hearts! So I came home and reread the scriptures to see if I was missing something. And to my surprise, I discovered a large measure of joy written right in the Bible. An Old Testament prophet announced, "The joy of the Lord is my strength." A Christmas angel announced, "Good news of a great joy" (Timothy 6:17). And a poor, single missionary from jail wrote to the Philippians, saying, "Rejoice in the Lord always."

Both the Old Testament Hebrew and the New Testament Greek use a number of different words for joy. When David killed the giant in battle, he returned home to a hero's welcome. The women met him "singing and dancing with joyful songs and with tambourines and lutes" (1 Samuel 18:6). The word here for joy is *simchah* and it literally means "bright and shining." If you have seen the eyes of a bride before a wedding, or a child's eyes on Christmas Eve, then you've seen this sort of bright and shining joy.

Another word for joy is *masos*, as found in Psalm 48:2. It means leaping and jumping for joy, not unlike a football team that's just won the championship. When Peter and John healed the cripple at the temple gate, the man went "running and leaping and praising God."

Psalm 126:6 uses *rinnah* for joy. This type of joy translates as exuberance and shouting. We hear some good news and our hearts respond through our mouths with a "Hallelujah!" or a resounding "Amen!" or "Praise the Lord!"

There is also Psalm 13:5 and the joy word *gil* which means "to move around in circles." Watch what happens when you unchain a dog and set him free to roam, or watch a snow skier on the slopes during his first morning run.

Old Testament joy is boisterous, leaping, bright shining eyes, noisy exclamations, or even the antics of running clownishly around in circles. And the Bible says God not only approves of such, he actually encourages it.

Three times a year God required Jews to venture to Jerusalem to worship in the temple. Psalm 33:1 and 3 tell how "it is fitting for the upright to praise him." "Sing to him a new song, play skillfully, and shout for joy!"

When David brought the ark to Jerusalem, he stripped himself to a loin cloth and went before the parade dancing. With bright shiny eyes, leaping and circling, and shouts of acclamation, he praised God.

The New Testament word for joy is *chara*. It is very close to *charis* or grace. The idea is that if one is saved by grace (*charis*) then he should experience *chara* or joy.

Look at the portrait of Jesus painted in the New Testament. Sure it has its somber tones — denouncing Pharisaism, weeping over Jerusalem, wincing at unbelief, and dying on a cross. But there is also the color of joy — wine at a wedding feast in Cana, taking time out to be with children. Luke 10:21 even tells us that during a time of intense conflict Christ was moved to sing a hymn of praise and he became "full of joy through the Holy Spirit."

What was the early church like? A persecuted minority, poor, and meeting in secret, Acts 2:46 still says they "ate together with glad and sincere hearts, praising God and enjoying the favor of all the people." Paul used the word joy sixteen times in his short Philippian letter written from prison.

It is against this background of rich biblical heritage that the church today must answer why we are so joylessly boring, so overly serious, and so somber. Instead of a community of joy we've become a community of sourpusses. We speak of fasting but never feasting. The sound of tambourines is replaced by complaining. And we justify ourselves by pointing to the specter of nuclear warfare, widespread famine, and the sins of a wayward generation. "Who can be joyful in such a world?" we ask.

I once traveled to south Texas to try to make myself useful at a Fellowship of Christian Athletes camp on the border. And never have I been to such a dull place! The towns are one-horse towns in which the horse has already died. And it's so flat that people pass by a fifty-foot rise in the desert and call it a mountain. And hot! Why, in April it was 97 degrees with humidity so high a breeze felt like a dog breathing on you.

The landscape was all tumbleweeds, mesquite trees, cacti, and 200 miles to anywhere. And I've never been to a place where so many things bite and sting: scorpions, rattlesnakes, and more spiders than you can shake a shoe at! And mosquitoes! Why, they're the state bird of Texas!

Barney and Sherry Sarver have been ministering in south Texas for over ten years. I spent five days ministering alongside them and found it fascinating. Barry explained to me how mesquite trees burn hot and long and thus help make the best barbecue. He got me up at 1:00 a.m. to show me a meteor shower. He fed me a chili pepper so hot I still sweat just thinking about it. He pointed out roadrunners and armadillos, Texas blue bonnets, and cactus flowers.

There was an electrical storm so bad I wanted to find a bomb shelter in which to wait it out. And Barney explained to me the differences between ball lightning, chain lightning, and heat lightning. He could look into the desert and see dozens of different plant species, look into the faces of children and say if they were Incas, Mestizos, Spanish, or Anglos.

And I realized something with him. It is possible in Jesus Christ to have joy in a hot, humid, flat, rural desert infested with the occult even after ten years of labor.

Most of us today confuse joy with happiness. Happiness comes from the same root as "happening." Thus, happiness is circumstantial. It depends on your happenings happening like you want them to happen. So to be happy we must spend all our times trying to arrange our circumstances so things will happen like we need them to so we can be happy. Are my stocks maturing? Are my children on the fast track for success? Did I have a good vacation? Is my car tuned? Does the new house meet my expectations? Is my weight just right? Is the business booming?

Two things here: One is that by the time I so arrange my happenings that they happen so I can be happy I am simply too tired to enjoy them. And, two, there are always at least one or two happenings that have the poor taste to get out of line and ruin my day. The children act up. The stock market crashes. I get a dent in my new car.

I preached at a singles' conference and a 29-year-old woman approached me to talk. She was lovely to look at, educated, wealthy, a Christian, enjoying the company of many friends, but totally unhappy because she had no husband. Just one thing was out of line, and she was unhappy.

Joy, on the other hand, is not circumstantial. It is based on God's presence and a moment by moment celebration of the gospel. Paul wrote of joy in Romans 5:2, 3, and 11. "And we rejoice in the hope of the glory of God. More than that, but we also rejoice in our sufferings ... we also rejoice in God through our Lord Jesus Christ, through whom we have now received reconciliation."

The Past

Three things here Paul says are fuel for joy. First, "We rejoice in God through Jesus Christ through whom we have now received reconciliation." This means there are things in our past that are cause for joy. God has redeemed us. The Greek for "received" is a bookkeeping term. For example, let's say I'm hopelessly in debt. $463,249.12 to be exact. I've lost my job, depleted my savings, the bank has foreclosed on my house, and my cars have been repossessed. Tomorrow I'll be on the street.

But then I receive a phone call. A rich friend calls to say, "I hear you're in real trouble. I can help. And I want to. I'll be right over with my checkbook. Don't worry. Leave it to me!" That is how it was with me and my sins. I was morally bankrupt, getting in deeper all the time. And Judgment Day was coming. Then Jesus came. "I can help," he said. "Put your sins on me," he soothed. "I can offer you my rich grace."

Hence, I can rejoice in my past reconciliation. With bright shining eyes, shouts of exaltation, and the antics of a clown, I can joyously celebrate being debt free in Jesus Christ!

The Future

Paul also points to the future as fuel for joy. He says, "And we rejoice in the hope of the glory of God!" The word for "hope" here means "overwhelming confidence." And our world is losing hers. In fact, few in our world handle the future very well. Doomsayers, survivalists, hoarders, alcoholics, party animals have all taken on the attitude, "Eat, drink, and be merry for tomorrow we fry, die, choke" or whatever particular blend of disaster they foresee.

I like watching the reruns of *Hawaii Five-O*. It's about a world of crooks, plots, guns, groans, lawlessness, and impossible odds. Yet no matter how bad things get, I know how it will end. McGarrett will triumph and say, "Book 'em, Danno!" And that's how the Bible says history will end. Christ will triumph. Good will win over evil.

The world sees only a hopeless end. In Christ, however, we have an endless hope, an overwhelming confidence.

So where is my fuel for joy? It's in a sense of what God's bookkeeping grace has done to my past. It's in what God will do in the future. And now Paul says joy is also to be found right here today, even in my present sufferings.

The Present

Most of our lives are like the beds we sleep on. The headboard is straight up. The footboard is firm. But the mattress sags in the middle. And our faith is like this. The headboard is our future and we are confident of going to heaven. The footboard is our past, and we do rejoice knowing our sins are forgiven. But our todays are sagging like a worn-out mattress!

Not Paul's! He speaks of his todays, saying, "Not only so, but we also rejoice in our sufferings." The Greek word for "sufferings" means pressure or stress. And for Paul, it was chronic illness, poor eyesight, singleness, rejection, disappointment, trouble with the law, the stress of responsibility, trying to write, and living on a tight budget. And can you believe it? Paul made the bold assertion that we each rejoice in such present sufferings?!

Now Paul tells us why. He says that "suffering produces" endurance, character, and hope. At Colonial Williamsburg I visited a blacksmith shop. The smith heated his forge white hot and thrust in an awkward-looking piece of metal. When it glowed red, he removed it to his anvil and hammered it into shape. This process he repeated several times until he'd fully refined it, hardened it, and shaped it into something useful.

When I came to Jesus Christ, I too was an awkward Christian — weak, shallow, unreliable, superficial. And God put me under the stress of suffering. Loneliness, rejection, poverty, tests, mental anguish, accountability, failure, enemies — I've known them all. Oh, the pain of being purged and broken and shaped! Oh, the agony of God's hammering, shaping, and strengthening. But I conclude as Paul does. Rejoice! Because suffering produces endurance, character, and hope. And thus, suffering is not something to be avoided but something to be embraced. It means you are growing up.

I'm convinced so much of the unhappiness and depression of our world today is theological at root. When German theologian Helmut Thielicke visited the United States, he commented, "The American people have an inadequate view of suffering." Our happenings do not happen like we want them to happen, so we pine away in misery. But beyond our circumstances is joy in knowing that God can grow us up even in a time of suffering.

Conclusion

I was jogging with a friend and we ran past a lilac bush. Spasms of fragrance swept into my nostrils and I stopped to enjoy it. My friend turned around and jogged back asking, "Is something wrong?"

"Smell that!" I exclaimed.

"Smell what?" he asked, mystified.

"Concentrate! Smell!" I urged again.

"Oh, that," he said dully.

You see, it is possible to get so busy making a living we forget to make a life. When we concentrate on arranging our happenings so that they happen the way we want them to happen, we can walk and run right past lilac bushes in full bloom and never even enjoy. But in Jesus Christ, the fruit of the Spirit is joy! And we've got time.

One Born Among Us

Have you ever noticed the importance children play in history? When King Henry VIII of England and his queen couldn't have a baby, he divorced her, made another woman queen, and tried again. No baby resulted. Desperate for a male heir, Henry divorced and remarried yet another time. By now the Pope of the Catholic Church said, "Enough!" So King Henry split with Rome and helped found the Anglican Church.

Babies also play an important role in painting. Who could ever forget the marvelous children painted by Mary Cassatt, the American impressionist?

And what about children in literature? Remember George Elliot's *Silas Marner*? A bachelor, old and miserly, finds a child asleep at his fireside. He takes her in and is forever changed.

A favorite story of mine is by Bret Harte. Born in Albany, New York, Harte moved west at age seventeen. There he began to chronicle the wild West in short stories. In 1868 he published "The Luck Of Roaring Camp." There men panned for gold, gambled, drank, and learned the art of quick fists and the fast draw.

Sally was the only girl in town. And she was everybody's woman. She got pregnant, but died in childbirth leaving behind a healthy baby.

Who was the father? The little one, indeed, belonged to all of the miners. So they decided to do their duty by the child.

But where would the child sleep? A miner went eighty miles over the mountain to fetch a rosewood cradle.

And what would keep the child warm? Wool blankets were too rough, so silk blankets were ordered. And how could a child eat beans and bacon and sourdough? They bought a cow for milk. And one of the miners took up farming.

And how could a child live in a filthy, rundown shack? Walls were painted, floors cleaned, and windows washed.

But, of course, no cursing, dirty miner could hold a baby! So the miners quit swearing. They took baths and began to dress better.

And how could a baby nap with the saloon piano blaring? With rowdy men shouting and brawling? A time of quiet was decreed each day so the child could sleep.

One day they decided to show the child the mines. Yet somehow the pit seemed too dark and dingy. So they planted flowers, put up street lamps, and planked the walkways.

Little by little, Roaring Camp lost its reputation for toughness and became a decent place to live. And so a little child born into a rough mining camp cleaned up the place. What a story! But sadly, it is fiction. Yet the Bible tells us a nativity story that is fact, the story of the birth of Jesus Christ.

Infant Jesus was born into our tough mining camp of a world. His was a world of mad King Herods, unjust taxes, a political rule of force and violence, prostitution, superstition, racial hatred, and drunkenness. And yet ... yet Isaiah prophesied that because Christ was born among us "The wolf shall dwell with the lamb, and the leopard shall lie down with the kid, and the calf and the lion and the fatling together, and a little child shall lead them...."

Diplomacy

When Christ was born, people settled their differences on the battlefield. Nations bullied one another. Might made right. Force and violence ruled the day.

Our nation struggled through a civil war 125 years ago. The Shenandoah Valley served as the breadbasket of the Confederacy and Lee's back door to Washington.

General U.S. Grant ordered Philip Sheridan to seize the valley and burn it so that a crow flying through it would find nothing to eat. So it was that little Phil came with over 30,000 Yankee soldiers. Rebel General Jubal Early opposed him with only 10,000 men. And for ninety days 40,000 men tried to kill each other.

The final place they clashed was Cedar Creek, Virginia. All night the Rebels had marched secretly around the Union left. Then, half an hour before sunrise, the Rebels attacked. With a scorching fire they charged out of the fog giving their chilling Rebel yell.

The Federals were shattered. Their line rolled up like a carpet. Four hundred raw recruits from New York made a stand on a hilltop. And this is what one soldier wrote in his diary about what he saw.

> *Here one of our boys, Anthony Riley, was shot and killed. His father Charles Riley was by his side. The blood and brains of his son covered the face and hands of the father. I never saw a more affecting sight than this: the poor old man kneels over the body of his dead son, his tears mingled with his son's blood. O God! What a sight ... Riley leaned down one more time, kissed Anthony's cheek, and joined his retreating comrades.*

During this tragic period of our nation's history, a young boy, child of a Presbyterian preacher, witnessed the aftermath of battle in a Confederate hospital. War's horrors deeply affected him. Later he became a Christian, the president of Princeton University, an elder in the church, and finally, the President of the United States. His name? Woodrow Wilson. Knowing war's awful cost, President Wilson kept us out of World War I as long as possible. Then he said we would "fight the war to end all wars." And to ensure people would stop settling their differences on the battlefield, he envisioned the "League of Nations." Man now had a new option — diplomacy, reconciliation, justice, a chance to talk it out, to turn the cheek, to go the second mile, to exercise self-control.

Diplomacy instead of war?

"And a little child shall lead them."

Slavery

When Jesus was born, most people were slaves. They were owned by another human being, treated as common property. Dehumanized.

Then in 1759 William Wilberforce was born to live his 74 years as an Englishman. A Christian, Wilberforce graduated from Cambridge and won a seat in Parliament at age 21.

By 28 he'd begun a campaign against slavery. Two years later, Parliament passed a bill condemning slavery. By age 33, the year was 1792, he got a bill passed which abolished slavery. Then in 1807 both houses of Parliament voted an immediate end to slavery in Great Britain.

Now Wilberforce worked to rid the British Empire of slavery. He worked tirelessly until 1825. Failing health forced his retirement from Parliament. He died in 1833.

Two weeks after his death, his bill became law. Where the British flag flew there would be no slavery. A 53-year struggle had ended in victory he never lived to see.

William Wilberforce, Christian and human rights statesman, is buried in Westminster Abbey, London.

"And a little child shall lead them."

Abortion And Infanticide

When Christ was born, abortion was practiced. So was infanticide. If an unwanted child was born, he or she was simply thrown away. The wrong sex, retardation, illegitimacy — all were ample reasons to get rid of a baby.

Antonio Vivaldi was born into the late 1600s in Italy. His hometown was Venice. Training for the priesthood, receiving ordination, Vivaldi found that he was not healthy enough to oversee a church. So he turned to music.

It was the practice of Venicians to throw their unwanted babies into the canals. Literally multitudes of their corpses could be seen floating in the water. So the church began an orphanage that took in unwanted babies. Vivaldi, the sickly priest, was hired to be the orphanage music teacher.

The school had as many as 6,000 girls in it. The forty best students formed an orchestra, and on Sundays and holidays it became popular for the townspeople to come out and see the children, led by their redheaded Vivaldi, make music.

Vivaldi wrote over 400 pieces for his girls. He died after 40 years of faithful service. He was penniless and unknown. His grave is unmarked.

"And a little child shall lead them."

Education

When Christ was born, very few people received an education. Most people learned a trade. Subjects like mathematics, history, philosophy, art, and medicine were beyond reach.

After the Roman Empire collapsed in the 400s A.D., the Dark Ages lasted for 1,000 years — superstition, illiteracy, and fear reigned supreme. Europe became all but unbearable. And many sought to come to the newly discovered Americas to begin anew.

Sixteen years after the pilgrims had landed at Plymouth Rock, a British Puritan preacher, John Harvard, came also. He became pastor of the Charlestown Church in Massachusetts Bay Colony. And it was his burning desire to start a school for the education of children. Sadly, John Harvard died his first year here at the age of 31. Yet he left his personal library of 400 books and half his fortune, 779 British pounds, to help found the school. Today Harvard University bears his name and is the home of the largest university library in the world. The school educates lawyers, doctors, professors, scientists, clergymen, even Christian politicians like Corazon Aquino, former head of the Phillippines. And what is more, Harvard has served as a model for the start of other schools like Princeton, Emory, Duke, Davidson, and the like. Ignorance?

"And a little child shall lead them."

Human Rights

When Christ was born, women had no merit in society. A rabbi of Jesus' day said, "It is better to burn the Torah than teach it to a woman." Females and children were little more than slaves.

During the European Industrial Revolution of the 1600s and 1700s, women and children worked eighteen hours a day under the most appalling working conditions. Their wages were literally pennies a day.

The rich got richer. The poor got poorer. And nobody said a thing.

When workers fell ill or suffered a nervous breakdown, they were simply discarded. Debtors went to prison. The insane were chained in unheated, rat-infested dungeons.

That's when Anthony Ashley Cooper, the Earl of Shaftesbury, was born. He lived for Christ 84 years, from 1801 to 1885. An Oxford College man, he secured a seat in Parliament for 25 years.

It was his mission to sensitize the social conscience of his nation, to argue responsibility, the compassionate use of wealth. He worked specifically to see that the insane were given humane treatment, and that women and children workers were not abused. It was by his efforts that the first laws were passed that limited working hours and ensured humane working conditions and fair pay.

Injustice? Oppression? Insensitivity? Lord Shaftesbury brought relief.

"And a little child shall lead them."

Ecology
When Jesus was born, people did not know the proper use of things. Human waste was dumped into the same river from which people drew their drinking water. Trees were chopped down for firewood with no effort to replant. Fertile soil was seeded, harvested, and replanted until it played out. Then it was left to erode.

As the population of the earth increased, so did pollution. Smog, chemical contaminants, oil spills, the clear cutting of rain forests, radioactive fallout, and the depletion of the ozone layer became critical factors.

In our generation the American Medical Society warns that eighty percent of cancer in the human body comes from pollution.

That's when Dr. Francis Schaeffer began to write his Christian theology. He pointed out that we are tenants in God's garden. We are to dress the earth and keep it, not rape and pollute it. "The great sin of modern man," he wrote, "is to act like ethics has only to do with human relationships and not the rest of creation." Schaeffer wrote the classic book, *Pollution and the Death of Man*, to call us to simplicity and responsibility.

I had the opportunity to have supper with Donald Hodell, the former U.S. Secretary of the Interior. I asked him about his underlying ecological philosophy. Secretary Hodell told me he was a Christian and that Dr. Schaeffer's book had helped him form his views and this was what he was striving to implement.

"And a little child shall lead them."

Conclusion

Thomas Morton, in his book *The Seven Story Mountain*, asks, "How did it happen that, when the dregs of the world had collected in Western Europe, when the Goths and the Francs and the Normans and the Lombards had mingled with the rot of old Rome to form a patchwork of hybrid races, all notable for ferocity, hatred, stupidity, craftiness, lust, and brutality — how did it happen that from all this, there should come the Gregorian chant, cathedrals, the poems of Prudentius, the commentaries and histories of Bede, Saint Augustine's *City of God*?"

The answer? Into the chaos of "Roaring Camp" a little child has been born. A child of prophecy — Isaiah foretold him. A child of reconciliation — in him the wolf would lie down with the lamb. A child of God. Jesus, the Son of God! Why, his very name means "The anointed one of God to bring health." A child of leadership — "a little child" — so easy to overlook — but he "shall lead them." Are you following?

Imagine that! The one who formed the universe took form right here among us. He became one of us that we might become one of his.

Poet Carl Sandburg wrote, "A baby is God's vote that the world should go on." In Jesus Christ, God has voted for us. And as with Wilberforce, Lord Shaftesbury, Schaeffer, Vivaldi, and Harvard, it is not our ability, it's our availability that counts. A sickly priest with musical skills, a parish elder who only lived 31 years, a persistent statesman who worked for something he never lived to see — each followed Jesus and made the world a better place to live.

"A little child shall lead them." Are you one of them? Are you following?

When A Halo Slips

Many things are written with all of the excitement of some fresh truth recently received. Other things are written from anger. And there is much these days in any pastorate to make one mad. Still other messages are delivered from depression. I'm convinced that the majority of preachers I know are over the edge into burnout. And what of this particular study? Where am I coming from? Today, I'm writing from a broken heart, a heart shattered by a fallen comrade.

If I had to name ten people who've influenced my life positively in Christ, my friend would certainly be one of them. I chose to go to the graduate school I attended at least partly due to his influence. I can still quote you sermons and illustrations and theology and humor I received from his life over many years. But now my heart is broken.

You see, the police came and arrested my friend. He was tried and found guilty of sodomy, statutory rape, and incest. There were enough charges to put him away for life! But a merciful court reduced his sentence to ten years. And right now he's doing time in a federal penitentiary.

I'm still in shock. I just can't believe it could ever happen to such a man of God! Then I recall David the king, "a man after God's own heart." And I recall his coveting Bathsheba, his adultery, and the murder of her husband Uriah. And I know it can happen to some mighty good people!

But what to do? What is our Christian obligation to our brothers and sisters in the Lord when a halo slips?

Quite often we Christians resort to hostility. In fact, the army of Jesus Christ is at times the only army in the world that shoots its wounded. When a young, unmarried woman in the church gets pregnant, many a community simply tears her apart with their tongues. And we can do the same or worse with divorcees, convicts, adulterers, cheats, and drunks. Fail and you're a dead man, as far as some are concerned.

Nathaniel Hawthorne's novel, *The Scarlet Letter*, is a powerful tale of adultery and heartache. Hester Prynne is forced to wear the scarlet letter "A" to mark her as an adulteress. The Puritan townspeople destroy her with their tongues. She is snubbed from social activities, openly taunted, devastated. Poor Hester lives with her small child at the edge of town, lonely and silently suffering.

That's one way we can respond when a halo slips — just get our kicks in, step on them while they're down. Yet another way is to practice indifference. Simply quit caring about them. Write them off your list. Don't go to see them. Don't invite them over to see you. Leave them out of your plans, your prayers, and your affections.

Way back in 1635 the good citizens of the Massachusetts Bay Colony reacted with outrage at the radical ideas of Roger Williams, a Christian minister. And he was banished from the colony in the dead of winter. Now remember, this was New England in the 1600s. There was no hotel down the street and around the corner holding reservations for the man. He was banished to die in the wilderness for his liberal ideas. And it was all done in the name of God by a group of Christians who had fled Europe to escape the very things they now did.

Yes, when a comrade falls, when a halo slips, we can grow hostile, or we can be indifferent, simply walk out the door, and never speak to him again. And such behavior is more in keeping with the spirit of hell than it is with the spirit of Christ.

But I will show you a still more excellent way: the way of love; a love that is patient, that bears all things, a love that never ends.

Speaking of situations just like that of my erring friend, the Apostle Paul wrote in Galatians 6:1: "Brethren, if a man is overtaken in any trespass, you who are spiritual should restore him in a spirit of gentleness. Look to yourself, lest you too be tempted." What Paul is saying here has nothing to do with hostility or indifference. He is counseling us to take the way of active love.

Let's look at his words more carefully.

First, Paul begins by addressing the church. "Brethren," he says. He is speaking to the household of faith. "Brethren." Brothers and sisters.

Next he says, "If." "If a man is overtaken in any trespass ..." Paul didn't say, "When," but "If." You see, sin doesn't have to be inevitable in any Christian's life. Our temptation and falling into every sin is not a forgone conclusion. But it is in the realm of possibility.

Paul next speaks of being "overtaken" in some sin. The Greek word here is *paraptoma*. It means "to slip up."

The imagery here is that of an icy footpath. One walks along, is not paying attention to his footing, and suddenly he slips and falls hard. It's that type of world, isn't it? In each of our paths there are stumbling blocks, slippery spots, and inclines into sheer temptation. And it is so easy to fall down.

In my friend's case, he had gotten out from under authority ten years ago. He'd left one ministry to form his own, developed a board of directors who met twice a year to rubber stamp his plans, and, with precious little openness to correction and accountability, hit the road doing his thing as a speaker. You can add it up from there. Lonely hotel rooms. Extended periods away from home. The pressures and temptations of our sex-rated society blathering lust at us from the radio, the television set, the billboards, and magazines. A weakening theology and resolve. Perhaps a fantasy here and there. An opportunity. A sudden fall. And another and another. Then a habit. Then Satanic oppression. Then jail. No. Not an easy world to walk in, this. Slippery.

Paul goes on to talk of our being overtaken in "any trespass." He doesn't narrow his concern to "some trespasses" or the "trifling variety" or such. He is wide open. "Brethren, if a man is overtaken in any trespass ..." You see, there is no unforgivable sin for the Christian. Not adultery, nor theft, nor lying, nor murder —

no, nothing! No sin in the Christian is outside God's grace and our concern!

Next Paul speaks to "you who are spiritual." Those who are steadfast are called to action. The strong are to care for the weak, the healthy are to minister to the wounded. And next Paul tells us how.

"Brethren, if a man is overtaken in any trespass, you who are spiritual should restore him in a spirit of gentleness." The Greek word for "gentleness" is often translated "meekness." It literally means "tamed strength." The word summons up one who is righteous and powerful, yet under control. You've seen those big Clydesdale horses like they use in Canadian logging camps. They harness them to huge logs and have them drag them out of the forest. But a Clydesdale is so gentle that a little child can play all about its feet with no threat of harm. That is meekness, gentleness, tamed strength. And that is the way we are supposed to go to our erring brothers and sisters.

Often when a brother is down we lose our temper, call him on the carpet, hold him up to public ridicule, and blow him away with both barrels of righteous indignation.

But Paul says that's not the way. "Strength under control" is the technique.

And now comes the really good news. Paul says one's goal in going to an errant companion is to "restore him." The Greek word for "restore" means to correct a fault or to heal. It is like a doctor restoring a broken leg by resetting the bone.

The really interesting thing about the word "restore" is that it is such a rare Greek word that it is used only one other time in the New Testament. In Matthew's Gospel the disciples are on the beach "mending their nets" when Jesus met them. The word "mend" is the same word as "restore." And what a beautiful parallel! Just as fishing nets get torn and need some mending, so do people. And just as nets can be mended to catch more fish, so can people be restored to useful service in the kingdom. Do you hear the Good News here? Anyone who fails and any form of failure can be forgiven and mended.

Now, I realize this Gospel is at odds with a lot of our thinking. You can see how we treat ex-convicts, Presidents who resign under a cloud of immorality, and slipped and fallen saints in the church, and see that we believe a person is worthy and useful until his first fall, and then he's had it, finished, benched!

H. Butterworth has a poem about all of this:

> *I walked through the woodland meadows,*
> *Where sweet the thrushes sing,*
> *And found on a bed of mosses*
> *A bird with broken wing.*
> *I healed its wound, and each morning*
> *It sang its old sweet strain;*
> *But the bird with a broken pinion*
> *Never soared as high again.*
> *I found a young life broken*
> *By sin's seductive art;*
> *And touched with Christlike pity,*
> *I took him to my heart.*
> *He lived with a noble purpose*
> *And struggled not in vain;*
> *But the life that sin had stricken*
> *Never soared as high again.*

That's a sweet poem. It brings a tear to one's eye. I bet you like that poem. But God thinks it stinks! He's just got one thing to say about birds with broken wings that never fly as high again — "Bull!" Did you hear that? "Bull!" Jesus Christ saves completely. He saves us from the guttermost to the uttermost!

When the Jewish nation turned from God and fell into sin, she was conquered and ruined. Her temple was leveled. But God brought his people back. And Haggai 2:9 prophesied, "The latter splendor of this house shall be greater than the former." In Joel 2:25 God promises, "I will restore to you the years which the swarming locust has eaten...." In short, the Lord can mend our lives, restore our nets to full service ever again!

Now Paul closes. In his last sentence he shares a warning to all believers. "Look to yourself, lest you too be tempted."

Aye. Here is a call to self-examination, to humility. "Don't enjoy it," Paul is saying. "Don't look down your nose at those in the family who fail. Let your knees knock, your heart ache, that Satan could ever claim such a trophy. Be quite conscious that you, too, walk a slippery path and will no doubt be tempted and are quite capable of the same evil at 21 years of age or at 51 or at 94!

During the mid-1700s a preacher in England watched as the executioner's cart rolled by carrying a convicted murderer to the gallows. The rowdy street crowd jeered the criminal and pelted him with stones. The preacher only turned to his friend and whispered, "There but for the grace of God go I." Yes, and so it is. "Look to yourself, lest you, too, be tempted."

During the tumultuous 1960s and the Civil Rights activity, Dr. Martin Luther King, Jr., discovered the dishonesty of a trusted aide. When the full implications of the man's crimes came to light, most of his staff advised King to expose the man, fire him, and make a public example of him. But Dr. King would have none of it! "The church," he said, "is in the business of forgiving, reconciling, restoring. The world gives us enough examples of ruin. We shall give them an example of mercy and healing." And so may it ever be! So may it ever be!

Today, in all our concern for the lost and fallen of the world, let us also include a little concern for those in the family who fail, and let us thank God for mercy, restoration, and reconciliation. For at one time or another we'll all surely need it.

I close with James 5:19-20, a beautiful promise for those who practice the ministry of reclamation. "My brethren, if any one among you wanders from the truth and someone brings him back, let him know that whoever brings back a sinner from the error of his ways will save his soul from death and will cover a multitude of sins."

Epiphany Of The Lord
Isaiah 60:1-6

Shine! That's The Style!

It is appropriate on this day designated as the Epiphany Of The Lord to explore some questions we might ask Jesus as the light that has come to the world. We'll be a panel of inquirers and we will let Jesus Christ answer our questions. We will call our program *Meet The Congregation.*

Who?

Our first question will be, "Who is the light of this world?" In Matthew 5:14 Jesus tells us: "You are the light of the world." Did you catch that? The finger is pointing at us. You are the world's light!

In John 9:5 Jesus said, "As long as I am in the world, I am the light of the world." And now Jesus looks at his followers and compliments them. "You," he says, "you too are what I am! Just as I shine as the light of the world, so you also shine as lights. People will look at you and they will not see darkness. They will see light!"

Now, who were those people Christ complimented so? They must have been special men and women! Who were they? They were common people like you and me. They were blue collar workers, simple fishermen like Peter, James, and John. They were tax collectors, government bureaucrats like Matthew. They were professional men like the physician Luke. They were construction workers, a tentmaker like Paul. They were housewives like Mary and Martha. And to them Jesus said, "You are the light of the world!"

The Church today has lost something of the wide significance of this text. "The pastor is supposed to shine," people say. "That's what he gets paid to do. But we church members, we don't have to shine. It's not possible to be the light of the world where I live and where I work." Do you feel this sort of thinking is rare today? Well, it is not! Just the other day a pastor introduced himself to a business man who responded, "Oh! You are a minister! You're one of those paid to be a Christian!" Now there you have it. Just like that businessman, many others today feel that shining as the light of the world is not for them. It is for the pastor. But it is not true. Jesus disagrees with this sort of segregated thinking. And as in the days of old, Jesus turns to all of his followers today and says, "You are the light of the world!" You are a lantern to guide people down the footpaths of life. You are a lighthouse to warn of danger. You are a friendly candle in the window to point the way home. You are the north star men guide themselves by. You are the light of the world.

Where?

So, who shines? You do! Another question we need to ask is: "Where do we shine?" Again Christ responds, "You are the light of the world." Where do we shine? In the world! Christ didn't say, "You are the light of the church." He said, "You are the light of the world," and that includes the office, the school, the factory, and the home! You are the light of the world wherever you go.

Many people say: "You know, pastor, I just cannot witness. I am too shy. I don't know what to say." But Christ is not inviting you to be a witness. He is not asking you to decide if this is something you want to do or not. He says you are light right now! You are the light of the world already. And whether you know it or not you have been witnessing for a long time! You witness in the way you pay your bills and order a meal in a restaurant. You witness in the way you drive a car, in the adjectives you use, in the way you treat your employees, and in the way you spend your Sundays. Your life witnesses even when you are not aware of it.

I was at a church banquet once. I had been invited to speak after dinner. And as I sat at the head table I suppose I was rather conspicuous. At any rate, the waiter had put a big slice of pecan pie beside each place setting. And since I love pecan pie and the main meal hadn't been served yet, I took my fork and ate a little piece of my pie. It was so good and I was so hungry I took a second bite. It was then that I became aware of a tussle going on between a mother and a little child seated at another table. The child was wanting to eat her pie before the meal and the mother was saying, "No, it will spoil your appetite!" Well, that little girl just pointed to me and said, "It's okay, Mama. He's eating his!"

Dear people, we need to realize that the light God has put in our lives cannot be hid. Jesus tells us, "A city set on a hill cannot be hid." God didn't light your lamp to hide it under a bushel. He puts it where it will be seen. It gives light to all in the house. When I was a small boy my family used to visit my grandparents in the mountains. We'd leave on a Saturday afternoon and return by Sunday night. When Sunday morning came, we did not go to church. We spent the time visiting with the family. Now my great-grandmother Mrs. Espy lived with my grandparents at the time. And she loved our visits. But when Sunday mornings came she went to church. I remember watching her prepare for church. She picked out her best dress. She put her shoes on with a great deal of effort because her feet were always swollen. Then she got her cane and headed for church. Once I remember her even going to church in the snow. How often as a child I watched her and wondered, "What is so important about church that she'd leave her family and go there? Why, if my feet hurt like hers I'd stay home. When it snows we stay home from church. Why does she go? Something she does there must sure be important to her." Yes, Mrs. Espy, you are dead and gone to be with Jesus now, but you were the light of your great-grandson's world. Oh, you never knew you were witnessing by what you did but there were little eyes watching you. You, Mrs. Espy! You were the light of the world! A city set upon a hill that could not be hid. Thank you for your faithfulness to me. I'm in church now come rain or snow, family visits, or slight illnesses. You pointed me to the church and the church pointed me to Jesus. You taught me faithfulness. And you weren't rude. You were the light of the world!

How?

Who shines? You do! Where do you shine? In the world! There in your homes, on the job, at play, and especially when your children visit. Either you shine or you do not shine! Now, is there another question you would like to ask Jesus about shining? Yes, there is! "Jesus, if we are the light of the world, how do we shine?" Christ's answer is, "Let your light so shine before men that they may see your good works." How do we shine as lights? We shine with good works!

It is true that good works do not save us. We are saved by the life, death, and resurrection of Jesus Christ. We are saved by our faith in what God has done for us. But because we are saved, because we are Christians, we do good works!

Look at the works Jesus did. He saw that the blind, the lame, the leprous, the deaf, and the dumb got medical treatment. He fed the hungry and pointed the way to the confused and lost. He saw that beverages were provided for wedding guests and taught a group of people to pray. Following Christ around is to witness one good deed after another. He literally laid down his life for others.

How about you? If someone followed you around would he see good deeds? Would he see you going the second mile, turning the other cheek, being a good Samaritan, and sharing a cup of cool water with the thirsty? Have you ever noticed how a boat leaves a wake? That's right. The path of a ship is marked by a wake sometime after it passes. Did you know that you leave a wake behind you? It's true! When you pass through the world each day you leave a mark on both people and things. You either leave people feeling agitated, depressed, and cheated, or you leave them feeling more hopeful and at peace. What kind of trail do you leave behind? Is it a trail of good works? The scripture says that Jesus went about doing good. And how often we Christians are just content to go about.

The Bible teaches that we are to follow Christ's example. Jesus said, "Truly, truly, I say to you, he who believes in me will also do the works that I do" (John 14:12). In other words, our lives must match Christ's. To call ourselves Christians and not do good works is like wearing a green striped shirt with blue plaid pants. Our character and our name wouldn't match. It wouldn't be in style! But here is what is in style this epiphany season for the faithful Christian! Good works!

Man alone cannot do good works like Christ. We cannot shine like this in our own strength. Consider the moon, for example. In and of itself, the moon has no power to shine. It is only a dull, barren ball of dirt. But when the sun shines on the moon it lights up. You and I are like the moon. We are barren, dirty people. There is no light in us. But we can shine when God sheds his light on us! We can reflect his light! And that is what happened to us Christians. God has removed the barrier of sin that blocked his light from us. There is no longer an eclipse. The Bible says, "For once you were darkness, but now you are light in the Lord; walk as children of light. For the fruit of light is found in all that is good and right and true" (Ephesians 5:8, 9). Brethren, do you hear this word from the Lord? Once you lived in darkness. God's light was eclipsed by your sin. But now Christ has removed that barrier. God's light shines upon us. And like the moon we reflect that light in good works!

Why?

So, who shines? You do! Where do you shine? In the world! How do you shine? By reflecting God's light in good works. Now we have one final question to ask Jesus before our show *Meet the Congregation* is over. "Jesus, we have asked who and where and how. Now we want to know why. Why do we shine?" And again the answer comes from Christ's own words. "Let your light so shine before men that they may see your good works and give glory to your Father who is in heaven." Why shine? So others will see and respond by giving God glory! In other words, we do not shine to brag about how good we are. The Pharisees did this. They wanted people to notice them when they did their good works. "Hey, look at me! I'm giving to the poor. See me putting money in the temple treasury? What a good boy am I!" But this is not as God would have it! Christ condemned the Pharisees for their self-righteousness. He told his followers to do good deeds but to do them so God would receive the glory and not themselves. The psalmist prayed, "Not to us, O Lord, not to us, but to thy name give glory" (Psalm 115:1). And this is what we are to do. We do not want people to believe in us. We want them to believe in Christ. We do not want people to praise us. We want them to praise God. We do not want people to say, "What a fine man you are!" We want them to say, "What a great God you serve! I shall serve him, too!"

If you are a person with a green thumb you have no doubt noticed how our houseplants tend to grow toward the sunlight. Plants will turn toward the window that lets light in. This effect is called phototropism. And this is the effect our lives should have on others. We should turn them toward the light. We should turn them to God. "Let your light so shine before men that they may see your good works and give glory to your Father who is in heaven."

So we have asked who, where, how, and why, and we have been told: "You are the light of the world. A city set upon a hill cannot be hid. Nor do men light a lamp and put it under a bushel, but on a stand, and it gives light to all in the house. Let your light so shine before men, that they may see your good works and give glory to your Father who is in heaven." You! You, the common followers of Jesus Christ, have been complimented by God today! The light of the world, the most beautiful man who ever lived, has pointed his finger at you and said, "You are the light of the world!" So, shine, Christian! Shine! That's the style!

What Does Your God
Say About People Like Me?

London, England, the Bloomsbury District, tenth floor of the old Ivanhoe Hotel, autumn, 1971. I was a young exchange student studying history, English literature, and such. Each morning as I looked out my window overlooking an alley, I noticed a dimly lit room in the apartment building opposite me. The windows were all sooted up. One pane was broken. And to keep the cold out someone had wedged a picture in the sash. Best I could see, it was the photograph of a man, very faded. Each day for three months I noticed that picture.

Often I still catch myself wondering about the man in the photograph. Who was he? Why did he live? And what circumstances caused his photo to be used as a temporary windowpane?

Do you ever feel like that? Out of place? Wasted? Fading away? Shoved into some ignominious hole?

So many in our world are like that: mental patients, refugees, prisoners, wards of a rest home, a business executive shoved aside in some merger.

Sociologists call us "the throwaway generation." We use and casually toss away bottles, cans, pens, razors, and ... people. Divorce ... abortions ... euthanasia ...

I was decorating the evergreen tree in my front yard one cold December day when a rattle-trap car bumped to a stop at my curb. Out comes a familiar looking face — Bobby — a former local college football star, big as a bear. In 1979 he was the best linebacker around.

"How are you?" I inquired.

And out of his mouth came a tale of woe. Unemployed. Mental illness. A lonely single. Nothing better to do than chain smoke and glue his days together with alcohol. Oh, the hurt! Oh, the wasted years! Oh, the loneliness! Bobby's question still haunts me. "What does your Book say about ruins like me? Is there any word from God?"

Yes, Bobby, there most certainly is.

Jesus said, "The Son of man came to seek and to save the lost" (Luke 19:10).

He Comes

If one visits the Natural Bridge of Virginia, one may see where George Washington, as a young surveyor, scratched his initials on the cliff wall. Indeed, George Washington was here!

Ah, but God Almighty was and is and is evermore here among us!

Deism is the belief in an absentee god. The Lord wound up creation like a clock and left it ticking in space. But he has walked away from it. We are abandoned. Yet, this is not what scripture teaches. Hear it? "The Son of man came ..."

He still comes ...

I made a tour of Israel once. I learned that Jesus, over his 33-year earthly ministry, traveled over 2,000 miles on foot. He was in Lebanon, in Egypt, and all over Israel. Why, every village, no matter how obscure, seemed to have had a visit by our Lord.

He came. And he still comes. Even unto you, Bobby. And to you and you and you.

He Seeks

"The Son of man came *to seek* ..."

In the cartoon, *Dennis the Menace*, young Dennis confides in pal Joey, "Don't ever play hide-and-seek with Mr. Wilson. You hide, but he doesn't seek!" Ah, but Christ seeks! In tiny villages Jesus walked. By the sea, at tax booths, by sick beds he sought people. Even on the cross he sought the soul of a dying thief.

And still today Jesus seeks the alcoholic, the infirm, the busy, the sinful. Even lonely tenth floor apartment dwellers peeking out

62

from behind broken windows stuffed with faded photographs. "The Son of man came ... to seek ..."

To Seek The Lost

Jesus said, "The Son of man came ... to seek ... the lost."

Isaiah foretold Jesus' coming. He said of Messiah, "A bruised reed he will not break, and a dimly burning wick he will not quench." There are two beautiful pictures here of what it means to be human and sinful and lost.

"A bruised reed" is a small musical instrument played by shepherds. It's made of wood, perhaps bamboo, and is played like a flute by rustics to pass the time on lonely hillsides as they manage their sheep. Such a "reed" is delicate. It can be dropped, sat upon, stepped on. Most musicians, upon breaking their flute, won't attempt to fix it. They simply throw it away. A new reed can be bought for pennies.

We fragile people can make music, too. But how often we become bruised. And straightaway we are shoved aside. Forgotten. Unwanted.

Isaiah says it's not so with Christ. He, rather, takes great pains to fix us, to restore us so we can sing his praises once more!

The second picture is of a "dimly burning lamp." You know, a lamp that offers more smoke than light. It fills the room with acrid smoke. It irritates the eyes. It is so aggravating you want to snuff it out!

Not Jesus. Even if we are an aggravation, more smoke than fire, more trouble than we're worth, he adds oil and trims our wick to restore our witness.

In short, when we're lost, he comes seeking. We're not castaways. He restores the light and music in our souls.

To Save

Now for the most beautiful of all Christ's promises. "The Son of man came to seek and *to save* the lost."

In the Greek "to save" means "to bring health." "The Son of man came to seek and to bring health to the lost."

In Christ's day Jesus was known as "Joshua bar Joseph." This was his Jewish or Hebrew name. How in the world did we get "Jesus Christ" out of that?

"Joshua" means "savior or health-giver." It was translated to the Greek language, "Jesus," for New Testament purposes.

"Bar Joseph" means "son of Joseph." It was dropped for the title "Messiah" in Hebrew, which translates in Greek to "Christ," "The Chosen One, the Anointed One."

Hence, Jesus Christ, the one God chose to bring health to the world.

This health God brings is in relationships with God. With people. With self. With creation. God's health is epitomized by love. You'll find the best description of it in the great commandment found in Mark 12:29-31. " 'Hear, O Israel, the Lord our God, the Lord is one; and you shall love the Lord your God with all your heart, and with all your soul, and with all your mind, and with all your strength.' The second is this, 'You shall love your neighbor as yourself.' " Such becomes a man or woman, boy or girl, who relates to Jesus.

So, I ask you, have you received this salvation? Are you discovering this health in your relationships?

Conclusion

In the mid-1960s color television came to West Germany. Radio, television, and the news media all heralded the coming of color. But on the announced evening, thousands of black and white television viewers called to complain they were still only seeing black and white. The broadcasting station had to explain patiently that the problem was with their reception. Unless they purchased a color receiver, they couldn't tune in.

And you? What of you and me? God is broadcasting Christmas live and in living color. Are you receiving it in Jesus?

Christopher Columbus Speaks!

Five hundred years ago a man dreamed of reaching the east by sailing west. He sought trade, honor, and souls for Jesus Christ. This is his story ...

(Taped Fanfare)

(Columbus walks to the front. He is old, somewhat stooped, stiff with arthritis. It is after his fourth and final voyage, a few months prior to his death.)

Never give up. Never, never, never give up! When God gives you a vision, when his call upon your life is plain, then let nothing deter you. Not wars, nor lack of cooperation, nor money, not your low-born estate, not friends who play you false ... nor even the vastness of the ocean and its endless bounty of the unknown.

My name is Christopher Columbus, son of Susanna and Dominico of the weavers' trade in the fair city of Genoa, Italy.

I made four voyages to the Indies, voyages of discovery. Just over 500 years ago now, it was. And some tell me you want to know my tale. If it be so, then I'm here to provide.

1453, it was. The Muslims captured Constantinople and cut off the only known trade route to the east with all its spices, silk, and other treasures. Though I was but a small child at the time, I remember how hard economic times pressed upon my family. My father often could not get enough wool to weave. So it was that the Mediterranean nations began to explore for a new route to China. And the thinking was that the sea route was safest and certainly lay southward around Africa.

I believed China could be reached by sailing west across the Atlantic. As yet no other seafarer had tried it and succeeded.

In many ways my discovery of America started in 1451 in church at the baptismal font when I was an infant. My parents christened me "Christopher." It means "Christ-bearer." And as I grew to manhood my name became a divine commission.

I do not know the date of my birth. We celebrated our birthdays in that time on the feast day of our patron saint. My parents in calling me Christopher were consciously naming me after Saint Christopher, the patron saint of travelers. And his feast day is June 25.

Now Saint Christopher was a giant of a man, a Syrian who lived just after the time of Christ. He was converted to Jesus by a hermit who encouraged him to continue seeking God. "How do I seek him?" the new convert asked. "Fast and pray," the hermit said. "But I don't know how," Christopher complained. "Then be helpful to God's people," the old man encouraged. "Find a river without a bridge and help people cross safely. In time God will reveal himself to you." So it was that Christopher went and found a river without a bridge. There he built a cabin and devoted his life to helping pilgrims cross safely to the other side. And in a life of quiet helpfulness to travelers, Christopher came to know God.

All through my childhood my namesake fired my imagination. Could I live up to Saint Christopher's example? Could I be helpful to people? I used to sit on the wharfs of Genoa and look out on the sea and wonder if I could travel across oceans. I'd even pray I could be the one who'd find a new trade route to the east, perhaps as my name means, bear the name of Christ to people who had never yet heard of his redemption.

My grandfather, Peter Columbus, used to tell my brothers and sister and me the story of Raymond Lull, a missionary to the Muslims in Algeria at Bougee. He'd been stoned and left for dead on the beach by Islamic believers. My grandfather and a fellow merchant happened upon the missionary and, discovering he was not dead, took him aboard their ship. The missionary, as he began to recover, sat up and prophesied. Pointing westward he said, "Beyond this ocean which washes the shores of this continent, there lies another continent which we have never seen and whose natives know nothing of Jesus Christ. Send men there."

Verses like Zechariah 9:10 and Isaiah 51:5 stirred my hankering to sail, to discover, to bear the gospel of Christ. "And he will speak peace to the nations; and his dominion will be from sea to sea, and from the river to the ends of the earth." "The coast lands wait for me, and for my arm they hope."

So it was I grew up carding wool in my father's weaving shop. But I knew all along I wanted to put to sea, to discover a trade route to the east, to live up to my name and be a missionary. My brother Bartholomew and I used to sail along the coast of Italy in a little boat our father had leased. We'd sell cloth or trade it for wine and cheese. By age fourteen I'd made my first long sea voyage to Chios off Turkey. Then at seventeen, with the economic plight of our family nearing desperation, I signed aboard a trader ship bound for England.

We got caught in a nasty little war and a French ship sank us with her cannon fire. Hurt and frightened, I floundered in the sea, found an oar, and paddled six miles to shore. A fisherman found me and for two weeks nursed my wounds.

As I recovered, I found I was in Portugal near Lisbon where my brother Bartholomew had gone to work as a chart maker. I'd also washed up at the very place where sixty years earlier Prince Henry the Navigator had set up a school of exploration.

For the next years I worked with my brother Bart in Lisbon making charts for sea captains and selling books.

There I read Marco Polo's books about his travels to China 200 years earlier and the rich civilization he found flourishing. I read of how the church tried to force him to recant of his fantastic revelations of life in China. His only reply was, "The half of it I haven't told you!"

During these years I continued to make sea voyages as far north as the Arctic Circle and south to the equator. I became a master mariner able to captain any ship, and as knowledgeable of the ocean as any man alive.

Once while walking on the beach near my home I found washed up on the beach a strange piece of carved wood and exotic plants the likes of which were not to be found in Europe. Surely they had drifted across the sea from some strange land!

That's when the idea began to take shape in my mind: that it was possible to reach the east by sailing west.

Since the time of Ptolemy, educated people knew the earth was round. Oh, ignorant sailors filled with superstitious fears still believed it was flat and if one ventured too far from the sight of land they would fall off the earth. Yet the Bible in Isaiah talks about God "sitting above the circle of the earth." And at Christ's coming, time will be morning in one place, noon at another, and yet night in another! Thus, even holy writ tells us plain the earth is a sphere.

So, why not sail to the west to reach China and her rich trade? It'd be out of harm's way from Muslim armies. It'd be shorter than trying to round Africa. And the riches would be fabulous!

I found out other ships had tried it but turned around after a few days. I determined to try for myself. But the ships and crews and supplies I needed were expensive. Only a king could afford it! And here I was, son of a poor cloth merchant, an Italian foreigner living in Portugal. How could I ever meet a king and sell him on my idea?

Week after week I went to church to pray about things. That's when the Lord provided another of his marvelous coincidences! And was she pretty!

As I was strolling home from church with my brother Bart, a young lady dropped her purse and I recovered it for her. Felipa was her name, a high-born lady of Portuguese society. I did like her from the first. And she must have been taken with me, for soon I was called to her house to sell books. I found out her father, a former governor, was now dead. So she lived with her mother and brother. We were allowed to court under the watchful eye of the nuns. I proposed marriage and was accepted. And at age 27, we were wed in the church where we met. A year later our son Diego was born.

Although I was now moderately prosperous as a book vendor and chart maker, I still hankered to put to sea westward on a voyage of discovery. Felipa did her best to talk me out of it. But I'd infected her whole family with my vision! And since my in-laws were well-connected politically, I was able to arrange for an audience with King John of Portugal.

He immediately appointed a committee to study my proposal. While holding me in suspense King John was secretly trying to reach the Indies by sailing around Africa.

So I waited and waited and waited. Months turned into years. Seven long years. Then in 1485, my thirty-fourth year, both tragedy and rejection struck me like two hard fists. Lovely Felipa took ill and died suddenly, and the king's committee pronounced my plans fantasy. To top it all off, I was nearly broke from the expense of living in and around the royal court.

Seven years of waiting! All for nothing! Widowed. Broke. And not just rejected — my plan was called a foolish fantasy. Oh, in those days I ached to give it up, to quit my vision for the secure life of a prosperous merchant. Yet there was my grandfather's tale of the prophet, my name to be lived up to, and my skill as a seaman. And surely I could never abandon all this and be fulfilled!

So I decided to leave Portugal and try for Spain. With my last money I reached the seaport of Palos in southwestern Spain. Little Diego and I knocked there on the doors of Rabida, a Franciscan monastery. We were given food and lodging. The monks agreed to watch over my five-year-old son and see to his education. And what's more, the monks listened to my vision and were enthusiastic about a voyage west to China and my desire to proclaim Christ. So they introduced me around in influential circles.

That's when I met a rich merchant who was willing to outfit a ship for my westward voyage. But at the last minute he backed out, citing how angry the king might become if he tried it and succeeded without permission.

So I was off to see King Ferdinand and Queen Isabella. I told them of my name and calling, of the vision that burned so brightly in my mind. And the queen was especially touched. She, too, was a Christian with a desire to fulfill the Great Commission to carry the gospel to the world.

Odd, looking back, how alike the queen and I were. We were both born in the same year, both redheads, both Christians, and both focused on missions!

But! It seems as if my life then was a tedious and frustrating procession of "Buts!" But Spain was at war with the Moors, Islamic invaders from Africa. But the war had wiped out the royal treasury. "But, of course, our scientific committee will have to study your proposal for some time." "But if you'll just wait ..."

I was 37 years old by now. And I was spending my whole life waiting!

Months dragged by into years.

I decided to try King John of Portugal again. He was more favorable, but just as he was ready to say yes, Bartholomew Dias returned from sea, having rounded South Africa to reach China. And it was all off for me in Portugal after that.

So I returned to Spain. My brother Bart wanted to try France or England for backing but I decided to wait out Ferdinand and Isabella.

During this time I remarried. Her name was Beatriz and in a year my second son, Ferdinand, was born.

The Moorish War dragged on and on. Then suddenly, January 2, 1492, it was ended! Spain had won, driving the Muslims from Granada.

The court reconvened, restudied my proposal, and after a delay of seven years, denied it. "Unrealistic!" they pronounced. "Unfounded." "Imaginary."

Fourteen years gone! Waiting! All to no avail! Wearily I mounted my old swayback horse and, broke, homeless, and in my one tattered coat, decided to try for King Charles of France. It was the lowest point of my life.

Ah! But God works in mysterious ways his will to perform! For the treasurer told the queen of my turn down, told her she was missing a wonderful opportunity with little to lose and much to gain. Whereupon she changed her mind, offering to pawn her royal jewelry if necessary to pay for the expedition. As it turned out, such wasn't called for. The treasury had the $14,000 necessary to fund the voyage west.

So a courier was sent out to find me. I was already out of town but he caught up to me and brought me back to court. There I was commissioned to set forth westward to the spice islands.

I decided to leave from Palos, the seaport west of Spain's Gibraltar. Three caravel sailing ships were put to my use. The *Pinta*, the *Nina*, and the *Gallega*, which I renamed *Santa Maria* or *Holy Mary*. A merchant who owed the king a favor had to put up his ships.

Ninety men soon signed up, outfitting and provisioning the vessels. We painted three huge red crosses on each sail. Then on August 3, 1492, in my forty-first year, the crew met in the church of Saint George in Palos to pray. The king and queen themselves were there to pray Godspeed to us. And I gave command, "Weigh anchor and proceed in the name of Jesus!"

We sailed southwest to the Canary Islands. There was a known steady westward wind available from those shores, also a last chance to take on water and food.

But near the Canary Islands the *Pinta*'s rudder slipped its hinges, I think a deliberate attempt by her owner to put the ship out of commission so as not to risk her on the voyage. Reaching the Canaries, repairs took three weeks.

While we were waiting in the Islands, a huge volcano erupted, belching out fire and illuminating the nighttime sky. My crew was afraid, seeing it as a bad omen. I told them it was only God Almighty showing us his power, a power that was for us, not against us.

Come September 6, repairs made, we weighed anchor and sailed west from the Canaries into uncharted western seas. For the next thirty days we held to a due west compass bearing. All the while I estimated our speed and position by dead reckoning.

The men were restless, afraid we'd come too far to make it back. I had to do my best to coax them on day after day.

At sunrise we gathered on deck to sing God's praises. I purposely forged a duplicate ship's log that grossly under-calculated the distance we'd sailed. When a head wind beat against us, a wind that nicely would have taken us home, it required all my skills to persuade the sailors to persist in our voyage westward.

Then came the day we sailed into the Sargasso Sea, "the sea of weeds." Right in the middle of the Atlantic! As far as the eye could see! The ocean was covered with sea weed! And there we were becalmed. The men were petrified. "Surely our ships will become bound fast and we'll starve!" I had to promise a rich reward if we sailed on.

October 7, 1492. A full thirty days at sea. No sight of land. The sailors were restless. Mutiny was in their minds. Then the shout, "Land, ho!" But to our bitterest disappointment, it turned out to be a cloud band low on the horizon.

It was at this point I had to strike a bargain with the crew. "Give me three more days. Just three days. If we do not make landfall in 72 hours, we'll go home."

Here again God was gracious. The *Nina* found a flower adrift in the sea. A sailor retrieved from the water a piece of wood with iron fastened to it. Then we saw a flock of birds. I quickly abandoned my compass heading west and sailed in the direction the birds took. That night, October 11, about 10:00, I thought I saw a light flickering on the horizon. Other sailors agreed. Then at 2:00 in the morning, October 12, clearly in the moonlight, an island appeared. Trees, surf pounding on a sandy shore. Land! This time it was no mistake!

Bedlam broke out on board. We raised our flags, fired our cannons, and sang hymns of praise. After 33 uncertain days at sea, we'd finally reached the Indies!

Come first light we moved closer to shore to investigate. That's when we first saw the Indians! Stark naked! Every one of them!

I donned my best clothes, a green coat and red cape, and with the Christian flag unfurled, led the shore party in. There I fell on my knees and thanked God for his mercies. And we claimed the land for Jesus and for Spain!

Looking back, I realize now how easy it would have been for the Muslims to have discovered America first and made it Islamic. And another mercy! Where we came ashore the Indians were friendly. The Taino Indians, as it turned out. It could have been otherwise. The nearby Caribs were cannibals. And the Aztecs on the mainland practiced human sacrifice. But we were spared.

The natives, Indians we called them, watched us from a safe distance at first. But we befriended them with gifts. They particularly liked our beaded necklaces and caps. Soon these strange people were swimming out to our ships.

The Indians were handsome, with painted bodies and short dark hair. We quickly noticed some had gold earrings in their noses. Soon we were introduced to smoking tobacco, parrots, cotton cloth, exotic fruits, and something called the hammock, which natives sleep in as it is strung between two trees.

I called the island we found San Salvador, meaning "The Savior." But since it was small, and clearly not the mainland of China or Japan, we followed the Indians' directions and sailed southwest for the land the natives called "Cuba."

Island after island passed by until we reached a huge land mass with fresh flowing rivers. That's when I realized our fastest ship, the *Pinta*, had sailed off and left us. Martin Pinson, the captain, had proven me false and, overcome with gold fever, had abandoned me to seek his own ends!

There was nothing to be done but go on. So for many days we investigated the shores of Cuba. Still finding no great Indian cities of trade, we sailed eastward, reaching another land mass which so reminded me of Spain I christened it "Hispaniola." Today it is known as the island of Haiti and Santa Domingo. There on December 24, 1492, after ten weeks of exploration of the Indies, disaster struck! In the night a storm wind caused the *Santa Maria* to slip anchor and flounder on a reef. She stuck fast, and we had to abandon her on Christmas day.

Safely ashore, but with only one ship to take us home, I decided to build a colony. "Navidad" or "Christmas," I named it. Thirty-nine crewmen agreed to settle it. And salvage from the *Santa Maria* would stake them until we returned on a second voyage.

So it was on January 2, 1493, I boarded the tiny *Nina* with my crew, said my good-byes, and sailed for home. No sooner had we reached open seas than we spotted a sail. Turned out to be the *Pinta* with her scalawag of a captain Pinson who just happened upon us. And together, with a favorable east wind, we made for Spain.

73

After thirty days at sea a horrible storm struck. For a full fifteen days Satan did everything he could to sink us before we could report our discovery. I so despaired of reaching Spain that I wrote down the details of my journey, sealed it in a bottle, and tossed it into the sea in hopes someone would learn of our fate. And we prayed to our God for deliverance.

That's when the storm began to lessen, and within a few days we found ourselves in the Azores Island group. The officials were amazed at us. Said they didn't know how we had survived. Said it was the worst storm they had ever seen.

It was March 15, 1493, that we returned again to Palos, Spain. For 32 weeks we'd been gone. A voyage of 224 days. I myself was ever so glad to be home. At 42 years of age, an older man in those days, I was moving slowly, stiff with arthritis.

And, oh, my! The sudden acclaim we received! I rode horseback across Spain to where Ferdinand and Isabella were in court. I was received as "Admiral of the Ocean Seas," made governor of all I'd reached, and asked to make a second voyage as soon as I could be outfitted.

In all, I made four voyages to the Indies. I could tell you of many adventures and sorrows. Adventures of crossing the Atlantic in 21 days, of the colony at Navidad being destroyed by Carib Indians, of a hurricane wiping out the later colony of Isabella, of how I explored South America, the Mosquito Coast of Central America, and the island, Puerto Rico. I could tell you how worms ate my ships on the fourth voyage, and how I spent a year and five days marooned on Jamaica. I could tell you of the joy of sailing with my sons Diego and Ferdinand.

Seems I was a good explorer but a poor administrator. Many in Spain, along with those who sailed with me, were smitten with gold fever. And the new colonies I brought them to were not making them rich quickly enough. Many wanted to quit for home. They derided me as "Admiral of Mosquitoes." During my third voyage a newly appointed jealous governor of the Isabella Colony had me put in chains and sent home in disgrace!

Here in Spain, I found my patron Queen Isabella had died, and King Ferdinand had lost interest in me. Most of the royal court found me tiresome, and all the promises of financial reward were forgotten. I was worn out, arthritic, and, for the most part, bedridden. Death would claim me in a few months in a modest house in Valladolid, May 20, 1506. I was but 53 years old.

Though I clung my whole life to the belief I had sailed to China, I remained confused as to where I had arrived. And it was a frustration to me and my countrymen that we could not find the rich spice countries of trade.

Looking back with the wisdom of 500 years of hindsight, I cannot honestly call what I did the discovery of the continents of North and South America. After all, the Indians were already there. Further, the Norwegian Lief Erickson and the Irish monk Brenaden were all in America before me.

What I did was encounter the New World and give a report of it to Europe. Times were such that my findings were recognized and acted upon. Thus the sea path between Europe and America was officially opened and commerce begun.

My life also serves to illustrate the two natures of man. Indeed I nobly sailed west to live up to my name — Christ-bearer! It was my heart's desire to evangelize the Indians. And from 1492 to 1820, Spain alone sent 15,000 missionaries to the New World, establishing missions from South America to Saint Augustine in Florida to the far west in California.

But the base sinful nature of our humanity also reared its ugly head. Gold fever and greed led to wholesale slaughter, rapes, and pillage of many Indians across America.

Yet in all this God was sovereign. The Indians gave Europe corn, tomatoes, rubber trees, tobacco, rice, and venereal disease. The Europeans gave the Indians Jesus Christ, horses, and fatal smallpox. In fact, over the next 200 years the majority of Indians were wiped out by European fevers. So, in the interchange between the new and old world, history-changing forces none of us then could either imagine or control were at work.

Hardly eleven years after my death Martin Luther was to begin the Protestant Reformation. And in the warring convulsions that resulted, many Christians saw the New World, so underpopulated, as a place to plant their new Christian communities. Scarcely

100 years after my discoveries, Puritans, Quakers, and Catholics were founding settlements built on Christian values. Certainly only a sovereign God could manage such a feat that would give rise to the United States and her constitutional example of freedom and the incredible vitality she has shared with the world in education, missions, free enterprise economy, and more.

At my birth my countrymen believed the best lay behind us. We looked to the past to discover our greatness. Hence there was little interest in the future, in science, in education or Christian reform.

Our flag had as its motto, "No more beyond!" But after my voyages the "no" was dropped and our motto affirmed, "More Beyond!"

As I leave, thanking you for hearing my tale, I challenge you with your own future. For certainly there is always more! More beyond!

As I had, may you have a good name, seek a vision from God, and though you suffer privation, set back, and endless waiting, if you but trust in God and persist, you will surely plant His flag on new territory! Never give up! Never, never, never give up! Though all men fail you, though you be poor, lowborn, and though your sea be vast and the wind against you, yet God is faithful....

Try This On For Size!

I have a friend who is a millionaire. He just built a huge new home and furnished it with fine antiques. He even bought a $30,000 grand piano. When I last visited him my three-year-old girl saw that piano, and since most children like to bang on pianos, she quickly climbed upon the bench and began to plunk away. Needless to say, her father quickly put an end to that! Only a master can touch a superb musical instrument like that!

Another friend of mine has a 250-year-old grandfather clock which was handcrafted in England. It stopped ticking recently. Well, what do you do when a priceless heirloom is broken? Do you call in the neighborhood tinker? Of course not! You call for the best clock repairman around!

Let's suppose your wife is ill. She needs delicate open-heart surgery. Maybe you made an "A" in high school biology, and successfully dissected a frog once. Would you operate on your wife in the kitchen? Of course not! You'd seek out a specialist! You'd take her to the best!

But how about us? What about ourselves? When something goes wrong with our lives, to whom do we turn for help? Do we go to a professional, a specialist, the master? No! We go to Bob or Jim or Sue or Carol across the street. We trust some amateur or the astrological charts or Jean Dixon or Dear Abby or Congressman so-and-so!

Jesus said, "Come to me." "Come to me all you who labor and are heavy laden, and I will give you rest." When we depend on an organization, we get what an organization can do. When we depend on psychiatrists and doctors, we get the best medicine can do. When we depend on government, we get the best government can do. But when we come to Jesus, we get the best God can do! One of the things I regularly ask people who come to me for help is, "Have you taken your troubles to Christ?" And invariably most say, "I've talked to my mother. I've listened to my friend's advice, even seen a therapist, but no, I haven't taken it to God yet."

"Come to me! Come to me!" Jesus says. When your life is broken, when you are weary or hurting and in need of repair, come to Jesus. He is the Divine Physician who can heal. He is the Master Repairman representing your manufacturer. And he will examine your life and fix it. Yes, "Come to me," Jesus says. "Come to me." He is the Master. He is the way, the truth, and the life. "Come to me."

Are You Tired?

Jesus also says, "Come to me all who labor and are heavy laden, and I will give you rest."

A German tourist was asked, "What impresses you most about the United States?" He answered, "The fact that you are a tired people impresses me a great deal. Clerks, wives, friends, teachers, youths, leaders, institutions — you are all so tired!" Could it be that he was right? Is America tired? Have we worked and schemed only to win the badge of fatigue?

Just look at our homes — count the divorced people around you. How many women are too tired to have a baby, so they abort? How many parents are too tired to rear their children? How many homes are no more than a laundry, a hotel, and a filling station?

The drugs we take also accuse us of being tired. "Pick-Me-Ups" are a morning must, a little "toddy-for-the-body" in the afternoon, and of course, the "tension reliever" at night. Did you know that it takes about eighteen million sleeping pills to put America to sleep each night?

Even our institutions are tired. Churches are lukewarm. They are becoming a "bless-me bunch" instead of a blessing. Our government is facing an energy crisis, law is tired and lax, art is tired and dragging, even our money is tired! The dollar doesn't do near what it used to do.

A more affluent society has never before existed. A healthier people has never lived. And a tireder race has probably never breathed. Listen to the words of a suicide note left by a young college boy:

> *Dear America,*
>
> *I'm tired. Tired of puppets instead of people, of people with long hair and denim coats, pot parties and fraternity pins, people who drop soliloquies carefully labeled intelligence. I'm tired of people who play the dating game like tips at the race track. I'm tired of seeing people used because it's only a game, of people who turn love into a social grace and women into a piece of beef, of watching sincerity fester into smoothness. I'm tired of cynics who label themselves realists, tired of minds rotting into indifference, of people bored because they are afraid to care, of intellectual games of Ring-Around-The-Rosy. I'm tired of people who have to be entertained; tired of people looking for kicks with a bottle in one hand and a prophylactic in the other; of girls proud of knowing the score and snickering about it, of girls intent on learning the score. I'm tired of sophisticated slobs, tired of drunkards and dopeheads who are never more than spaced or tight, of people who tinker with sex until it's smut, of people whose understanding goes no deeper than "neat" or "cool" or "sharp." I'm tired of people who scream they hate it, but won't leave it because they are lazy, tired of people with nothing better to do than glue their days together with alcohol or dope. I'm tired of people embarrassed at honesty, at love, at knowledge. I'm tired. Yeah, very tired. So long.*

Could it be that any of you are tired like the young man in this letter? How about you? Are you tired? Jesus invites you, "Come to me all you who are tired and heavy laden, I will give you rest." The Greek work for rest is better translated "relief." "I will give you relief." The Christian life is not a rest from any and all struggle, work, involvement. It is a gift or relief so one may devote his energies constructively.

The prophet Isaiah (40:28-31) was speaking to a tired people when he said:

> *Have you not known? Have you not heard? The Lord is the everlasting God, the Creator of the ends of the earth. He does not faint or grow weary, his understanding is unsearchable. He gives power to the faint, and to him who has no might he increases strength. Even youths shall faint and be weary, and young men shall fall exhausted; but they who wait for the Lord shall renew their strength, they shall mount up with wings like eagles, they shall run and not be weary, they shall walk and not faint.*

Where are those in our community who are old but who have come to Jesus, who have waited on the Lord? I'm thinking of Moses leading the Exodus in his eighties; a man like the burning bush, he was ever burning but never consumed. I'm thinking of middle-aged Dorcas, the woman who did so much with her needle and thread. Where is she today? And there is David, the young shepherd boy with a slingshot. And where is young David today?

Yes, it does look like America is coming and going to everyone and everything but Jesus. And we are a tired people. And that's why Christ's words are so relevant. But Jesus isn't for everyone. He doesn't call for everyone. He only calls for the tired and heavy-laden. He's not calling for the self-sufficient, for those who can get along quite well without him. He calls only for those who feel a need. "Come unto me all who are tired and heavy laden," he says. "I will give you relief."

The Yoke

Jesus also says, "Come to me, all who labor and are heavy laden, and I will give you rest. Take my yoke upon you, and learn from me; for I am gentle and lowly in heart, and you will find rest for your souls. For my yoke is easy, and my burden is light."

80

Notice that Jesus gives two commands and a promise. The commands, "Come to me," and "Take my yoke," are what make the promise, "I will give you rest," come true.

Also notice that Jesus says that we must be saved *from* something *to* something. This should not surprise us. God saved Israel *from* Egypt *to* the promised land. He saves us from the flesh to the Spirit. Jesus says we need to be saved to his yoke. How about you? Are you saved from your sins? But better still, are you saved to the yoke of Christ?

When Christ spoke of his yoke, he was speaking as a skilled tradesman. He was flashing back to his boyhood days. You see, Christ was a carpenter for twenty years or more before he turned preacher. His father Joseph taught him the trade. Together they ran a little shop in Nazareth. It was located in the poor side of town, down some inconspicuous, dusty little avenue. But it was a pleasant shop, well kept and nestled beneath the shade of olive trees. From it could be heard frequent peels of laughter amid the sound of hammering and sawing. The smell of fresh cut lumber filled one's nostrils as one entered the vicinity. And out front, legend has it, there hung a sign which read, "Our yokes fit well."

According to tradition, Joseph and Jesus made the best oxen yokes to be found. Even though their shop was inconspicuously located, people came from villages all around just to have their yokes made by Joseph and Son. They would tie their big oxen to a tree, step inside for a few moments, and soon emerge with a young boy. The lad would walk over to the oxen and take careful measurements. Then a lightweight wood was chosen; carving and filing was done. Finally there would be trial fittings. The yoke must fit just right. It could not be too tight, too rough or heavy because it would gall the animal's neck. And that would never do! Such suffering would inhibit the oxen's work. With Joseph and Jesus, you see, it was a matter of reputation, a matter of quality. The yoke must fit perfectly.

And now in the later years Jesus no longer fashions yokes for animals. He now makes them for people. And likewise, these yokes fit well. They are smooth and light of weight. In fact, they are tailor-made!

Remember all those hand-me-downs you wore when you were growing up? Recall the second-hand shoes that pinched, the dress that almost fit, and the shirt that was too tight? Well, God will never treat you like that. He'll give you a tailor-made yoke! Here, try this on for size!

God has a plan for every individual's life. He has a job for you to do. And better than anyone else, you are qualified to do it. In fact, if you don't do it, it won't get done, or it will be done second best.

What is your yoke in life? What is your calling, your ministry? Ask God! Seek him! If a man really wants to know God's will, then the Lord will surely find a way to show it to him.

Consider the man Saul. He'd taken upon himself the yoke of Phariseeism. But God sought to remove it and place on him the yoke of Jesus. Saul resisted. And on the road to Damascus Jesus blinded him and said, "Saul, it is hard to kick against the goads, isn't it?" To realize what God was saying to Saul one has to know that behind each ox team were sharp pointed sticks called goads. When an ox tried to kick his way out of the yoke he hit the points of the sticks and very quickly settled down. And likewise it was hurting Saul to resist the yoke God was placing on his back. But when Saul finally accepted God's yoke he became Paul and was given a life that fit him just right! He became the Apostle Paul, missionary to the Gentiles from Israel to Rome.

Many of you have found it hard to kick against the goads as you resist Christ's yoke. You are tired; you're weary. You've been saved from your sins but you haven't been saved to anything. "Take my yoke," Jesus commands. "Learn from me! For my yoke fits well!"

Saved From/To!

Did you hear about the young dog that was spinning round and round in circles? An old dog sauntered up to watch. "What are you doing?" he asked. "I'm chasing my tail," the young dog replied. "You see, happiness is in my tail. When it wags, I'm happy. When it droops, I'm sad. Happiness is in my tail! If I can catch it, I'll always be happy!" So again he spun round and round trying to catch his tail and bite hold of it. Finally, all out of puff, he sagged to the ground, tired out. The old dog, still watching all this, said wisely, "You know, I used to chase my tail. But one day I found out that if I just went about my business, happiness followed along right behind!"

Today Christ's invitation goes out to any of you who've been chasing your tail and are worn out. You need only come to Jesus. He will give you rest. He will save you from your sins to your yoke. And when you go about the Lord's business, happiness follows along right behind!

What's All The Fuss About?

Micah is the sixth minor prophet. We call the prophets writing in the last ten books of the Old Testament *minor*, not because their message is of less importance, but because they were brief. *Major* prophets are long-winded. *Minor* prophets preach briefly. Get the picture?

The name "Micah" in Hebrew means "Who is like unto God." Our modern names Michael, Michelle, and Mike derive from it. Oddly enough, Micah used his own name as the theme of his book. His brief seven-chapter, six-page prophecy is all about what God is like and how we can be like him.

Micah lived in the eighth century before Christ. Ministering during the reign of three different kings (1:1), he was careful to write down his sermons. It will help you to understand that the book of Micah is not one sermon, but a collection of short oracles or condensed messages preached over a lifetime in varying situations.

It will further interest you that Micah followed both Amos and Hosea as Israel's prophet. He was also a contemporary of Isaiah, their books sharing many similarities.

Micah was from Moresheth, a small village about thirty miles southwest of Jerusalem. His town happens to be on the main coastal caravan highway where there was much going and coming, so he would have grown up with a fair knowledge of world news.

Micah's outline is easy to follow.

1. Chapters 1-3, the failure of Judah and Israel to be godly and the prediction of God's judgment.

2. Chapters 4-5, the prediction that one will come who is god-like, the Messiah.
3. Chapters 6-7, pleading with the nation to lay hold of godliness.

Furthermore, 2 Kings 15-20 gives one the historical background of Micah. God had from old desired to reveal himself to a people. So, God began by selecting the Jewish nation. He freed them from Egyptian slavery, gave them his law, and gave them a land.

It was God's desire that Israel live in community, keeping his law, loving both God and people, establishing justice. God would prosper them; the nations would see and want such order for themselves. And they would thus come to know God.

I call this plan "window dressing." You can see it applied on the modern car lot. There the dealer places his finest automobile, washed, lighted, surrounded by music and adroit car salesmen. The idea is you'll see it, want it, buy it, and tell admirers where you got it.

God's plan worked well at first. The Queen of Sheba in Africa traveled to Israel to meet King Solomon and to worship his God. "The half of it wasn't told me!" she said of his great reign.

But Israel grew slack in her covenant with God. They wanted a king like the other nations. They took shortcuts morally. They married outside the faith; false worship crept in. Their religion became a convenience. They took God on their own terms and they began to treat one another abysmally.

This is when the prophets, among them Micah, appeared. Read 1:6-7 and you'll get an idea of his message. God will make his nation Israel "a heap in the open country." From a bright red, air-conditioned family sedan shining invitingly on the showroom floor to "a heap," a rusted-out, faded, and unwanted wreck of a car in a kudzu jungle. That's the picture of Israel.

Clearly God is saying he'll remove Israel as a nation because of the embarrassment of having His name associated with a corrupt people. He said the same thing to the churches in Revelation 1-3. Jesus called us "the light of the world." But when our ways are darkness, God promises, "I will remove your lamp stand."

The trouble with Micah's audience is they were in denial. "We're not that bad!" "Who's to say God speaks through you?" "Get a life, preacher! Don't be so serious!" "The good Lord will never do that to us!"

Like any preacher who takes his calling seriously, who feels he's being dismissed unheard, Micah turns up the volume. He becomes dramatic. Chapter 1:8 says he walked around Jerusalem barefooted, stripped nearly naked, and weeping openly.

Micah also used humor on his audience, particularly the pun. In chapter 1:10-13 he preaches, "Tell it not in Gath." "Gath" sounds like the Hebrew word for "tell." So, Micah is saying, "Tell it not in tell city." Next he cries, "In Beth-le-aprah roll in the dust." "Aprah" means "dustiness." So his word is, "In the city of dustiness, roll in the dust!" Then he cries, "Those who live in Zaanan will not come out." "Zaanan" means "to march" or "go out." So he is saying "Those who live in go-out-city will not go out."

To contemporize it, Micah's ploy is like me proclaiming that America's sin is so bad that Pittsburgh really is the pits, Washingtonians need to wash, and Wisconsin is living up to its name — Wiscon*SIN*.

Now for the clincher! The prophet shaves his head bald and invites others to do the same (1:16). You see, when foreign armies conquered a nation, they shaved the heads of the vanquished. Such not only shamed their victims, it provided easy identification.

"Get ready," Micah was preaching. "God's judgment looms! The Syrian army is on the march. They are the rod of God's anger!"

Go ahead! Read Micah, the naked, weeping, bald punster so intent on being heard. Very carefully he will share specifics of what's upsetting God about Israel's behavior. And through its message to our Jewish brothers one may hear his word to us, as well. It's all there — greed, lack of stewardship, a religion that only tells people what they want to hear, and leaders who use their position for self-serving gain. Micah decries a culture, not unlike our own, built on distortion, bloodshed, and wickedness.

After describing Israel's slide into sin and political collapse into exile, Micah softens. In chapter 5 he predicts a coming Savior, Messiah. "But you, O Bethlehem ... who are little to be among the clans of Judah, from you shall come forth for me one who is to be ruler in Israel, whose origin is from of old, from ancient days" (5:2). Eight hundred years later this very scripture was to guide the wise men to Bethlehem in their quest for Jesus' nativity.

Recall Micah's outline?

1. Israel is ungodly and doomed.
2. A Messiah who is god-like will come.
3. A final plea for God's people to be godly.

This brings us to chapter 6:1-8. God invites his people to plead their case with him. "If you've got a problem with me," God says, "spit it out! But know of a surety, I, God, have a beef with you!" Then God takes them on a brief history tour reminding them of his plans for them and of his strong deliverance over the course of the years.

Now comes what God is after: God-fearing behavior. Micah 6:8 is the most famous quote in the book. Some of you astute students of presidential history will recall James Earl Carter of Georgia, sworn in as President of the United States, had his Bible open to this verse in 1976. "He has showed you, O man, what is good; and what does the Lord require of you but to do justice, and to love kindness, and to walk humbly with your God?"

Aye! Here's what God is after — your walk with God and people. A walk with God that is humble and dependant, a walk with people that is kind and just.

Until that is a reality in each of our lives, we can expect to hear from Micah.

Let Sleeping Dogmas Awake!

There are many doctrines in the Bible that receive light billing today. Though the Bible is not silent on the matter, the pulpit is strangely mute. Which of you has heard a sermon on sleep? Indeed, we spend one-third of our lives in slumber; yet even though the Bible speaks of our nocturnal habits, few ministers preach on the matter. The same goes for other dogmas such as hell, meditation, tongues, and, of course, that which the text mentions, fasting!

Today, let us seek to remedy at least one portion of this abysmal situation and open the book on fasting.

What Is Fasting?

In the Greek," fasting" is *nesteuo*, meaning "not to eat."

Three sorts of fasts are taught in scripture.

1. The normal fast. This is to abstain from food, solid or liquid, except for water for a set period of time. Matthew 4 describes Christ fasting for forty days in the wilderness.
2. The absolute fast. This is to abstain from food and drink, including water, for three days. In Acts 9:9 Saul, after being blinded on Damascus Road, resorted to a total fast for three days.
3. The partial fast. This is to restrict one's diet in some manner, such as giving up sweets or meat. It represents self-denial. Matthew 3:4 explains such habits in John the Baptizer's life. And Daniel 1:15 says it was a portion of Daniel's life also.

Who Fasts?

Is fasting for you? Or is it a form of spiritual discipline no longer relevant? Scouring the scriptures, one compiles a list of fasting adherents that reads like a Who's Who in the Testaments.

Moses is the first recorded person in scripture who fasted (Exodus 34:28). King David fasted when Saul perished in battle (2 Samuel 1:12). Others who practiced fasting include the prophet Elijah, Daniel, the seer (Daniel 9:3), Nehemiah the builder (Nehemiah 1:4), Job the sufferer, the children of Israel (Judges 20:26), the people of Nineveh (Jonah 3:5-7), Anna, Hannah, Esther (Esther 4:6), and the apostles (Acts 9:9). Jesus even fasted (Luke 4:2). And great stalwarts of the later church such as Luther, Calvin, Knox, and Wesley fasted.

Now for the question ...

Should Christians Fast Today?

Jesus said in Matthew 6:2, 5, and 16, "When you fast ..." He did not say "If you fast ..." but "when." Furthermore, in Matthew 9:15 Jesus explained, "When the bridegroom is taken away, then they will fast." Clearly Jesus expected fasting to be a part of our spiritual discipline.

Now, for another question ...

What Happens When One Fasts?

Our physical bodies are like that of a camel. We can store up food and water in our inner pantry. But when we begin to fast, several things start to occur.

1. The body begins to use up excess fat.
2. The body is purged of toxins. A sort of physical "spring cleaning" goes on.
3. One has an extra three or four hours a day to pursue spiritual matters since one doesn't have to prepare food, stop to eat, or clean up three times.

During a fast the volume of the physical world is turned down, while the volume of the spiritual world is turned up. This is at least partially because the oxygen and blood normally going to one's stomach to aide digestion go instead to one's brain, thus aiding clear thinking. Carnality is diminished. Spirituality is increased. Self-control, a fruit of the Holy Spirit, is matured (Galatians 5:22). And one enters a period of greater sensitivity to Jesus.

You've, no doubt, heard the saying, "The way to a man's heart is through his stomach." Satan knows it's true. He used food to tempt Adam and Eve. Esau sold his birthright for a mess of porridge. The Hebrew children went to Egypt for food. God warned Israel against eating their fill and forgetting Him in their new homeland.

Jesus even predicted eating and drinking to the full would be a sign of his return (Luke 12:45, Matthew 24:37-38). So, Christ warned, "Man shall not live by bread alone, but by every word that proceeds from the mouth of God" (Matthew 4:3-11).

So, when we fast, we set food aside for a while to focus on God.

This engenders several splendid things!

1. It allows our digestive system to rest. By fasting one day each week your stomach will have nearly two months rest a year! And just as we rest our eyes or feet or minds, so we can rest our digestive track.
2. It allows us extra time to seek God.
3. It increases our spiritual sensitivity.
4. It fosters self-control.

Now for a fifth question ...

When Should One Fast?

Let's not become legalistic! The Pharisees fasted regularly for an outward show of piety. For them it was rote and devoid of spirit.

Simply fast when God moves you to do so. It is a matter of individual conscience.

In scripture, here are some examples of when God's people made the choice to fast.

1. For national repentance (Joel 2:12, Jonah 3:5, 10).
2. During a crisis (Jehoshaphat, 2 Chronicles 19). Paul blinded (Acts 9:9).
3. When power to intercess in prayer was needed (Nehemiah 1:1-11, Ezra 8:23).

4. Before big decisions (Acts 13:3, 14:23).
5. To return to the Lord (2 Samuel 12:7-17, Psalm 69:10).
6. For health and healing (1 Samuel 30:11-15, Acts 9:9). There is an interesting 3,700 year old Egyptian papyrus that quotes a physician, saying, "Man eats too much. He lives on only a quarter of what he consumes. The doctors, however, live on the other three-fourths."
7. To seek God's revelation (Daniel 9:2, 3, 21, 22; Acts 10:10).
8. To free the captives (Mark 9:29).

Now, for a final, sixth, question ...

How Do I Get Started Fasting
As A Spiritual Discipline In My Life?

Let me make a few trenchant suggestions. Begin with the book, *God's Chosen Fast* by Arthur Wallis. Next, go through the scripture references and read each one. Next, pray asking the Lord to show you what he wants from you. Begin slowly. Partially fast by missing a meal. Graduate to a 24-hour fast. And take it from there. God will show you.

Conclusion

When one goes to war, he must not forget his weapons. And fasting is a forgotten part of our spiritual arsenal. Let's pick it up. Let's choose what God has chosen.

Transfiguration Of The Lord
(Last Sunday After Epiphany)
Exodus 24:12-18

Do The Old Rules Still Apply?

Grandma was well into her eighties when she saw her first basketball game. It was a high school contest in which two of her great-grandsons played. She watched the action with great interest. Afterwards everyone piled into the van to get some ice cream, and a grandson inquired, "Grandmama, what did you think of the game?" "I sure liked it fine," she chirped. And then a little hesitantly she added, "But I think the kids would have had more fun if somebody had made the fellow with the whistle leave the players alone!"

I wonder, when it comes to God's law, do most of us feel the same way? We'd all enjoy our lives much more if we could do away with the rules!

Yet think two minutes about playing a basketball game with no rules: Anything is fair. Trip, gouge, cut, shoot, elbow, slug, even kick! A little of that and soon the game would become chaos. And players would be walking off the court in disgust, refusing to play in a game that is no fun!

The same with playing by the rules of life. Israel was a slave in Egypt when God through Moses freed them to become a new nation. Then at Sinai the Lord gave them the Ten Commandments with this introduction, "I am the Lord your God who brought you out of the land of Egypt, out of the house of bondage." "I freed you," God said, "and now I give you these simple laws to keep you free!"

Very simply, the Ten Commandments are a fence God places around our behavior inside which the good things of life can run wild.

Looking at God's law, it is immediately noticeable they were written on two tablets of stone. So the law is divided into two parts. The first four laws deal with one's relationship with God. The next six deal with one's relationship with people. In this sermon we will deal with the first four.

Priority

Law one reads, "I am the Lord Your God. You shall have no other gods before me."

"I am," God affirms. "I exist!" and, "I am the Lord *your* God." Straightway we learn God exists, and he is a personal God calling us to a relationship with himself.

Malcolm Muggeridge, the fine British intellectual, journalist, and author, became a Christian late in his life. When asked why, he explained, "I didn't want a God. I was not looking for God. But I had to come to terms with the fact that God wants me and came looking for me."

That's exactly what Adam and Eve discovered. When they sinned, they turned from the Lord to themselves and hid from God. Yet the Lord walked in the cool of the evening and called out, "Where are you?" And God sought the twosome until he found them. "I am!" God intoned, "and whether you like it or not, I am your God!"

You see, God is not broccoli that you may decide if you want him on your plate or not. God is God, the most important fact of the Universe. And God calls us to relationship with himself.

"I am the Lord your God. You shall have no other gods before me." Actually, the Hebrew word for "before" can also be translated "beside." "You shall have no other gods before me or beside me." God simply asks that he be our number one relationship, our first priority.

Many years ago, I was sitting in a movie theater with my girlfriend. We were watching James Michener's *Hawaii* when the main character wept to his wife, "I have sinned, because I love you more than God!" Immediately I was smitten by the Holy Spirit in my heart. By that time in my life I was a Christian. I loved the Lord. It's just that I also loved my girlfriend, football, clothes, money, myself, cars, and half a dozen other things. And, frankly, God was fifth or sixth down on my list of priorities. The result was, I was unhappy. So was God. And God was calling out to me like an anguished lover.

Try this experiment. Go home and turn your radio on. Tune it to a beautiful symphony with long stretches of pristine harmony. Enjoy! Now, turn the tuner dial just a tad to the right so that you're still receiving the signal, but you're also mixing it with another channel along with some static. The raucous sounds will cause you to do one of two things: either tune in or cut it off! That's what Jesus meant when he said, "No one can serve two masters." "You can't serve God and mammon." God wants our first love with no rivals, no static, in full tune. All other loves of our life aren't even close!

Is that how you love God now?

No Fixed Image

Law two requires us never to make a graven image of the Lord God and bow to worship it. It's with a great sense of relief that we come to this law, because most of us think we're not about to break it. But look twice!

Precocious Nancy, in the first grade, sat in her Sunday school class hunched over her drawing paper working eagerly with crayons. "What are you drawing?" the teacher inquired. "I'm drawing a picture of God!" the child confided. "That's silly," the teacher said. "No one knows what God looks like." To which the child replied, "They will soon!"

We laugh, but we all still think we've got God's picture. Ancient man experienced God in his conscience and through nature. He was awed. The Lord had a voice of thunder, the strength of a bull, the bosom of a mother, and the wisdom of the aged. So ancient man tried to symbolize God by creating a statue of him. Trouble was, when humans reduced God to an image, soon they elevated their image to the status of God. And it became a snare.

Though not many of us make statues of God and bow, often we have fixed inner conceptions of who God is. Many today see God as a grandfatherly figure, tolerant, busy, who likes baroque music, the sort of mahogany found in church pews, and big theological words like "ecclesiastical." In other words, God is an Episcopalian gentleman ... or Baptist ... or Pentecostal ... or, you fill in the blank!

Fact is, no human can ever fully conceptualize God. That's like trying to capture the Pacific Ocean in a thimble! Even the Apostle Paul was humble here. In 1 Corinthians 13, he wrote of knowing God, saying, "Now we see through a glass darkly." Paul is saying we view God through a very dirty window. Yes, Jesus said, "If you've seen me, you've seen the Father" (John 14), but still, of all God is, we know but the dimmest outline. Of his love, his grace, his wisdom, his holiness, his majesty we cannot completely comprehend. So law number two requires us to remain humble, to worship God open-endedly with ever-expanding wonder and awe!

Many years ago in the Louvre Museum in Paris, I watched a school teacher take her class of six blind students up to the famous Venus de Milo statue. The students felt the smooth white marble contours of the statue's feet and marveled at what all of it must be. And in a real sense we worship the Lord just like that. We know him. We have a grip on him in Jesus, but God is so magnificent and we are so small. There is so much to see and our vision is through a dirty window.

Is God for you a neatly packaged theological concept you've entirely figured out and stacked on a closet shelf marked, "Irrelevant for daily life"? Or is God a growing, consuming, emerging, relevant deity you can't learn about enough?

Reverence

The third commandment reads, "Thou shalt not take the name of the Lord thy God in vain." In the Hebrew, to take God's name in vain means to say it idly, emptily, with no sense of reality.

You have a name. And when you hear it called, you turn to the person calling and give him your attention. Aren't you disappointed when the person who used your name did so out of mockery?

Jewish people know God as Yahweh, a name so holy that it is unspeakable. God's name must never be used without a deep reverential sense that he is listening!

Today in Jewish courts, when a witness is sworn in, the judge says, "Remember, the earth trembled when God spoke the third commandment."

There are two major ways we violate the third commandment today. One is profanity. I watched a movie in which Jesus Christ's name was used quite regularly. But they weren't talking to my Lord. And how many of us salt our conversation by telling God what to damn and such? Profanity is basically trying to establish my own authority at God's expense. It reduces God's name to a swear word. It destroys reverence.

The second manner in which we violate law three is in lip service. We call Jesus Lord, then live as we please. We sign our name into covenant "in the name of God," then keep it only when it is convenient. We stand before the Lord and vow to wed in the name of the Father, Son, and Holy Spirit, in sickness and in health, for richer or poorer, for better or worse, till death us do part. Then we divorce when something better comes along or we get tired of trying.

And soon neither our words nor our vows or prayers mean anything. Reverence is completely destroyed by our easy familiarity.

Law three brings back the spine-tingling awe of the reverent use of language to and about God.

"Our Father." "Jesus." "Holy Spirit." "Almighty God." "The One Who hears me speak." When you say these words do you mean them reverently?

Sabbath

The fourth law reads, "Remember the Sabbath day to keep it holy." The Hebrew word sabbath means "to desist." Remember the day to desist and keep it holy.

Pharaoh's cruel taskmasters had put Israel to forced labor seven days a week, literally worked them right into the ground. So when Moses liberated them, God sat them down at Mount Sinai and said, "You are not slaves. You're my children. Work, to be sure! But take a day off, a sabbath to desist, to rest. And keep it holy! Keep it separated unto the Lord."

When I went off to college I had to learn to wash my own clothes. That means you let everything you have get dirty and piled up in the bottom of your closet. Then you wear it for six more weeks. Finally you decide to wash because it is hard to catch the foxes when you smell like the hounds. So you bundle everything up, walk to the laundry, open the lid of the washer, and drop it all in together — jeans, tennis shoes, white shirts, red plaids. And it all kind of swishes together in soapy suds and comes out grey.

That's what happens to life when we treat the Sabbath as just another day. We no longer keep it holy, separated unto God, so it is secular — just another day to work, run to and fro, play a game, sleep. And what happens? The bright, crisp, holy white of the Lord's presence in our lives grays until there's no knowledge of God in our lives or in our culture.

In the mid-1800s an English safari made its way into the African interior. For six arduous days the explorers and their bearers slashed their way into the jungle's heart. Come day seven, the leaders were up early to be at it again. But their porters wouldn't pack up. No amount of coaxing or threats would make them move; finally the black tribal leader explained, "Day seven we stop here and rest and let soul catch up with body."

There you have it. Refusing to let the material outpace the spiritual, allowing the spiritual time to grow amidst the secular.

Look at it this way. If I want to obey law one and put God first, and if I want to be careful how I conceptualize God and expend my physical energy bowing and pursuing him, and if by law three I am careful with my tongue not to destroy reverence as I talk about God, then there is only one thing more I lack — time. Time to put God first. Time to bow down. Time to think, to study, to talk of him in worship. Hence, remember the day to desist, to keep it holy, separated out from the rest of human affairs like work and shopping, traveling, etc. A day set aside for rest and worship that I might know God.

Conclusion

My friend, if you break the laws of agriculture the crop fails. Break the laws of architecture and the building collapses. Break the laws of health and your body suffers. The same with God's moral laws, the Ten Commandments. Just look around you today and you will see in our society the results of our breaking these first four commandments.

But here is the good news! While the law tells us what man must do, the gospel tells us what God has done.

Man has sinned. But God has come to redeem. Man has turned from the law to go his own way only to end up in ruin. But Christ has come calling us to turn back to God. And in the end he paid the penalty for our sins on the cross.

A student said to me, "Why did Jesus die on the cross? Why didn't God just forgive us? I mean, after all, he is God. He can do anything he wants!" I told the student God does love us. But his nature is also just. God loves us with the love of a judge.

I was riding in my car through the little town of Ware Shoals, South Carolina. I was doing about 45 mph in a 35-mph zone and a policeman coming toward me pulled me over. He said, "You're speeding. You're under arrest. You'll have to come with me." And he took me to the local justice of the peace who was also a barber who was shaving a man at the moment. He told me, "Sit down. The court will be in session in a few minutes." Sure enough, when he finished shaving the man, he stepped over to a desk in the corner, rapped a gavel, said, "The court's in session. What's the charge?"

"Speeding," the officer accused.

"Guilty or not guilty?" the judge asked me.

"Guilty, your honor, sir," I said.

"That'll be $65," he said, without looking up.

So I reached in my wallet to get my money to pay the man, when suddenly the judge looked up, stared at me, and a look of recognition crossed his face.

"Don't I know you?" he inquired.

I said, "I hope not, your honor!"

"Aren't you Stephen Crotts, the minister who spoke to our South Carolina State Fellowship of Christian Athletes convention?"

I said, "Your honor, sir, I regret to admit, that's me."

He stood up and said, "Put her there, pal!" And shook my hand vigorously. He went on to say how much my sermon had meant to his son, how our nation needed more preachers like me, and how welcome I was in his town.

Well, I slipped my wallet back into my pocket and felt relieved. He offered me a Pepsi and a pig's knuckle and we chatted amiably for thirty minutes. Then I reminded him I was in a hurry, after all, that's why I was here in the first place. "Another town in which to preach the gospel," I assured him. And as I turned to leave, he said, "That'll still be $65!"

Now he liked me. He was my friend. But he was still a judge. And what sort of judge would he have been if he'd winked at the law?

The crime had been committed. The penalty had to be extracted. So I paid dearly.

And what of this universe, God's law, and our lawlessness?

What God has done is take three $20 bills and a $5 bill and put them in the drawer himself. You've broken the law. But I'm going to pay the penalty for you.

That's what it means when Jesus died for our sins. He suffered the death penalty for sin we deserved.

All of us have sinned and fallen short of the glory of God. We deserved to die, to be separated from God forever.

But Christ stepped in and took our place.

All we can do now is turn from sin to God by faith and ask Christ to save us. But then God does a wonderful thing. God not only forgives us, he fills us with his Spirit and causes us to want to obey him, to live out his law — not to save us, but because we are saved.

Perhaps there is one of you here today who'd like to get in on this gospel. Right now, right here, you'd turn to Jesus and accept his grace and devote yourself in gratitude to putting him first, worshiping him spiritually, and using your days to reverently know and speak of him.

My friend, the old laws still apply!

SECOND LESSON SET

Holy E-Mail
Sermons For Advent/Christmas/Epiphany
Dallas A. Brauninger

Access To High Hope
Sermons For Lent/Easter
Harry N. Huxhold

Acting On The Absurd
Sermons For Sundays After Pentecost (First Third)
Gary L. Carver

A Call To Love
Sermons For Sundays After Pentecost (Middle Third)
Tom M. Garrison

Distinctively Different
Sermons For Sundays After Pentecost (Last Third)
Gary L. Carver